Fount OF • Blessings

One Survivor's Story of Healing and Redemption

D.T. CHRISTIAN

PAGE PUBLISHING, INC.
New York, NY

First originally published by Page Publishing, Inc. 2019

ISBN 978-1-64462-336-7 (Paperback)
ISBN 978-1-64462-337-4 (Digital)

Printed in the United States of America

In dedication to my dearest friend Bill who was a great example of loving others like Jesus would. He was one of my biggest encouragers and someone I want to emulate in many ways. His generosity was lavish, his spirit joyful, and his heart beyond measure. Even though he's gone to be with our Heavenly Father, his memory continues to touch many lives. Love you brother!

Loving thanks to my family and friends who have been my greatest supporters through this process and in life. You are a true blessing!

FOREWORD

As I begin writing this book, I've just passed my forty-fifth birthday. I can still remember back to a day when I couldn't even imagine being thirty, let alone forty plus. I'm not entirely sure how I got from there to here. Inside I think of myself as being about ten years younger than I really am. Maybe it's a delayed acceptance of the inevitable—something like my mind and body are in two different time zones. It's interesting to note that it didn't really start until after my twenties. Guess it didn't occur to me before then to look back at times past. I was only focused on my future. Then my kids came along, and that changed how I looked at everything.

However easily my self-image lags behind reality, there are definitely some changes happening to my body that cannot be ignored. In particular, there are two truths that I've come to accept at this stage. The first is that hormones are what they are and that they do as they please without consulting me. I mean, there is no rational explanation or quick fix when they start to go haywire. I don't even recognize the signs most of the time until I'm two days into a funk. I've had to resign myself to the fact that I can only do so much to deal with mood swings, night sweats, and foggy memory. Fortunately, I did find a supplement that helps tremendously. But this has been a raging problem for ten years, and all that the doctors tell me is that I'm not in menopause yet. Great. Something to look forward to.

The second truth I've come to revel in is that taking naps can be rejuvenating. It may sound indulgent, but I simply function better with some extra sleep. I've learned to appreciate the quality of my efforts rather than the quantity. By only working part-time, I'm able to give my best efforts to the people and causes that are most precious to me. Giving myself permission to infuse some down time into my day has improved my energy level for all the things I'm called to be. I'm a gentler parent, a diligent worker, and a more doting wife. Now that my kids are older, I even manage some volunteer hours each month. You can't argue with results.

What I'm getting at is that I'm coming to know myself better as I age. I wish that I could tell every coed what I now know about self-esteem. I am more comfortable in my skin now than I was in my twenties, wrinkles and all. I have new strength and determination that have grown as my spirit has come alive. The transformation has been very much like a butterfly emerging from its cocoon. All this wonderful change has occurred over years of living, learning, and yes, struggling. How did I get here?

Another truth I have realized is that people tend to be stationary in our personal development unless circumstances push us toward change. I actually have a self-improvement-driven personality—not the kind that pursues multiple degrees and achievements, but more like the kind that would rather recognize my own flaws and work on them than have someone else abruptly bring them to my attention. Let's face it; we can be our own worst critics. Yet despite this self-awareness of sorts, there were still issues inside me crying out for help that I was in denial about or simply didn't have the strength to conquer on my own.

Thankfully, there is a resource available bigger than any problem that I face and wiser than all the self-help books combined. Hopefully you know—it's God. And He's not like a dusty book waiting on the shelf. He pursues us and has a plan for each of our lives. His plans are to help us prosper, not harm us, to give us hope and a future (Jeremiah 29:11). This promise isn't meant to only manifest itself in eternity. I believe that there is so much more that God wants to do for us, not to mention through us, in the here and now. It can be hard to always recognize His goodness for the worldly standards of wealth and prosperity. Many tend to think of blessings in external terms, and they can be. However, God likes to work from the inside out. When we are able to focus our thoughts beyond the physical to the spiritual, we soon realize without a doubt that His plans are far greater and more fulfilling than anything this world has to offer. His goodness is like a drop of water on our souls that sends ripples of warmth and joy permeating throughout our being and beyond. Why does He offer us such compassion? So that we can pass that same comfort along to others (2 Corinthians 1:4). When we are blessed by His presence within, the blessing multiplies and spills out on those around us as well.

Introduction

Although my generation hasn't experienced a world war or a recession to the depths of the Great Depression of the 1930s, we have ourselves endured some national tragedies. I was in high school when the space shuttle *Challenger* blew up just after takeoff. I can still picture the disturbed look on my teacher's face as he entered our classroom and said, "We won't have class today. Find something to do on your own." His stark, somber demeanor let us know that something very bad had just happened. However, it wasn't until after that period, in the halls, that the news began to spread. Every one of us felt some sort of connection because this mission was supposed to have been the first to have a civilian science teacher on board. Her name was Christa McAuliffe. The media had been following her story for months, leading up to this historic moment. We as a nation were greatly anticipating the event.

Personally, I remember the sickening feeling of disbelief when I found out. Later in the day, I saw news footage of the takeoff and Christa's family looking on from the bleachers. As they watched the events unfold, their expressions of elation quickly changed to confusion then devastation. It all happened in a matter of seconds. I still can't begin to imagine the depth of their grief. It seemed that the sudden sting of reality must have stung worse after the excitement leading up to that moment—something like the way your stomach leaps at the crest of height on a rollercoaster then drops sickeningly as you descend. Only this wasn't a thrill ride. It was an unimaginable horror that slowly set into our realities over the following days and weeks. What that day taught me was how suddenly life can cease, literally, in the blink of an eye. It greatly affected me and our entire nation.

Eighteen years later, as a chaperone for my oldest daughter's eighth-grade trip to Washington, DC, we toured Arlington Cemetery. One of the memorials that we were privileged to visit was the commemorative gravestone depicting all seven *Challenger* crew members lost on January 28, 1986. Up until this point, I viewed each monument pretty much the same as the kids, with respect and wonder, but with no personal attachment to the depth of meaning behind the memorial. With this site, however, I felt a definite connection that these students didn't have. Even though I wasn't at the crash site all those years ago, I had experienced the event along with the whole country. It was a memory for me. Seeing the grave stone rekindled feelings of somber loss now intermixed with honor and pride for the crew's bravery and sacrifice. I was compelled to share their story with the students around me.

There was another tragic event that hit a bit closer to home on April 19, 1995. It was the Oklahoma City bombing. My family is rooted in the southern region of Missouri, a mere three hours away. On that day, I was working as the director of a childcare facility where I also brought my one-year-old daughter. One of the parents dropping off their child asked if we had heard the news. They told us that a van filled with explosives had erupted in front of a daycare center. We later found out that it was the Oklahoma State Building that was bombed, which included an on-sight center for children of employees. At first, I again felt disbelief. Then a sickening mixture of shock, fear, and sadness sank deeper and deeper into the pit of my stomach. I remember arriving home to an updated news report of the damage and devastation. I just stood in front of our television, sobbing, until I couldn't take anymore and turned it off.

Several things went through my mind. As a young mother, I could imagine how distraught and horrified the parents of those children were feeling. The amount of destruction was beyond my comprehension. I wondered who would do this and why. This kind of thing didn't happen in our country. My pain began to turn to indignation. I was sure that terrorists had struck on American soil and equally convinced that "we" would send a clear message that this would not be tolerated. When it was revealed that it was a rogue group of our own citizens that perpetrated this heinous act, I could hardly believe it. The truth was both sobering and sickening. Once again it was proven that our lives and our society can be turned upside down in an instant.

The third tragedy that I will mention is surely familiar to most who might be reading this book. It was the frightful day of 9-11-01, when terrorists struck areas of New York, Pennsylvania, and Washington, DC. I was out, running errands, as the details of that dreadful morning unfolded. After sending one daughter off to school and dropping another at preschool, I was headed to the veterinarian's office with our family cat and my one-year-old son in the back seat. Just as I was pulling out of the preschool's parking lot, the news of a plane crashing into one of the World Trade Center towers came on the radio. At the vet's office, I saw news footage of the plane striking the high-rise. The tragedy and impending loss of life was shocking. At this point, we all thought there must have been a malfunction with the airplane. We watched and listened intently for any explanation of what went wrong.

By the time the second plane hit the other tower, I was witnessing the unfolding events from my living room. There was also a report of another plane crashing into an empty field in Pennsylvania. What was going on? Reporters had no idea if the events were all related but doubted it could be coincidence. Later it was revealed that a fourth plane had crashed into the Pentagon building. Surely everyone watching felt powerless just like me. All we could do was hope and pray for an end to the devastation. The reality of terrorism that most US citizens felt confidently protected from within our borders was now our own. In light of these latest attacks, there was no more denying that life as we know it is not as secure as we would like to believe. Our everyday lives that we take for granted are more fragile than we care to think about.

For days, weeks, even months, the damage of this day kept playing out. Mounting stories of lost loved ones, fallen heroes, bravery among the chaos, and lives left shattered continued to pour forth. The wreckage was massive. This attack was a huge wound to our nation and her people. We slowly began to move forward with as much courage and hope as a country can muster. But on an individual level, we still felt numb with disbelief. We were fearful of what the future might hold. Somehow, though, we managed slowly and somberly to rebuild and keep living.

One thing that I found interesting was the way this tragedy drew us together as a people in purpose and intent. Just months prior, one of the leading news stories was about someone disputing prayer and the display of the Ten Commandments in our schools. They claimed that hearing God mentioned in public was offensive to them. Yet where did we turn when our stability began to crumble? One nation under God turned their faces upward and cried out. Many news crews and public officials, including the president himself, publicly requested or offered prayers for the victims, their families, and the future of this country. I never heard any complaints about that.

As a matter of fact, on that same field trip to Washington, DC, that I mentioned earlier, I noticed that God was woven throughout the principles and truths that this nation was built on. God was openly cited in official historic documents and on monuments honoring our leaders and fallen heroes, and mentioned in numerous quotes by respected men and women throughout history. It seemed clear to me that our country was founded by believers and established to be a God-fearing one. Why we would ever want to stray from that foundation is beyond me.

Just as significant as the shift in national focus was, at that same time, I had a personal experience of epic proportions. You would naturally expect that in light of events unfolding the morning of 9-11, my individual life struggles would fade into the background. And to some extent, they did. However, as I sat at that stoplight, absorbing the shocking news over my car radio, I became keenly aware of something equally as terrifying. There was a duality of emotions going on inside me. I could detect two distinct but very similar feelings all at once. It was in that moment that I realized the same intensity level of shock and devastation that was coming over me then was already present from the night before.

Chapter 1

I quite literally felt beside myself. As I dutifully ran my necessary errands that morning, I was reeling inside with personal torment. Just the night before, I had experienced one of the worst nightmares I had ever had. Although I was holding it together enough on the outside to function, my insides were numb and traumatized. My body was going through the motions, while my brain was frantically trying to get a grip on something rational. For the moment, that was taking care of my three young children.

If you were one of the billions following the news on 9-11-01, you know what I was feeling because all US citizens were reacting with the same emotions. Only for me there were two distinct sets, again nearly identical sensations, except one set was framed as a member of a nation under attack and the other was my own private hell. As details of that tragic day began to be unveiled, confusion and disbelief were replaced by much grief and fear. I know I felt afraid of what might come next, what I couldn't see coming, and how painful whatever it was might be. These were valid fears for the nation and for the personal turmoil churning inside me.

For as long as I can remember, my emotions have run deep and strong. That it could be any different never occurred to me. It was just how I was. Over my childhood, I was often told that I was too emotional and that I wore my heart on my sleeve. I didn't even understand what that meant. Did your parents ever say to you, "You better stop that crying, or I'll give you something to cry about"? Even as a young child, I realized how senseless that sounded. I obviously already had plenty to cry about. In all fairness, I don't recall the details leading up to any of these confrontations. And it wasn't just my parents, but also teachers and other "well-meaning" adults. These are just experiences that vividly stand out from an early age and definitely shaped my learned behavior. Unfortunately, it also greatly damaged my self-esteem and caused me to question my own sanity at times.

By the time I was in high school, I had learned to keep a lot of my feelings bottled up inside. That's also when I started picking at my own weaknesses and trying to "better" myself to avoid painful judgment and scorn from others. Of course, this wasn't a healthy solution. I suffered with deep anxiety, leading to an ulcer and panic attacks. When my emotions did come out, they were explosive and messy. I was extremely self-conscious and desperate to find acceptance. My only value came from good grades and having a boyfriend to validate my worth. And when none of that was working, I struggled with suicidal thoughts. The only thing that kept me alive was the fear of going to hell if I killed myself. So I kept pulling it back together, juggling all the broken parts of me the best I could and trudging forward in life.

There were for sure some happy moments too. Marrying my husband and having each of our three beautiful children are the highlights. Yet despite the happiness, the mess of a person I was on the inside kept coming up to the surface over and over again. It strained my marriage, made it hard to keep up with the pressures of working full-time, and tainted my parenting. I was still struggling with anxiety and depression, which worsened when life got hard. Troubles in our marriage finally led to couples' counseling. We were blessed to have a wonderful counselor at our church that was a great fit. Of course, it wasn't always smooth sailing. At the end of our first session, he told us that our relationship could be repaired and be better than it ever was. That made me furious because it was a lot of pain that had brought us to that point. Honestly, I wanted to slap him upside his head—hard. However, what I did was adamantly declare that I would never be thankful for what had brought us there, no matter how things turned out. The counselor was very gracious about it and made no further comments. That grudge remained in my heart for several years. In time though, God would prove me wrong. It's amazing how He uses even the littlest of details to get our attention and to widen our perspective.

On another visit, as we were discussing our families of origin, the counselor breached a bold question. He asked me if I knew of any sexual abuse from my childhood. I just shrugged my shoulders and quipped back, "Not that I know of, but if you could hypnotize me, maybe we'd both know." What an odd response. Don't you think? Although I had no conscious knowledge about anything of the sort, my subconscious was obviously suspicious. Again the counselor handled it with grace. Without flinching or a change in his tone, he simply stated that I exhibited traits of someone who had been abused. He never pressed me to talk about it any further.

The behaviors were just things that I thought everyone did. Things like compulsively locking the bathroom door when I took a shower and keeping the curtains of my bedroom drawn because someone might be watching me. It was also commonplace for me to have scary dreams of being chased or attacked. Often I felt paralyzed and couldn't fight back. At some point in my childhood, I began taking back some control of my nightmares by allowing myself to become invisible or shrink down to hide. However, that didn't work with my paralyzing dreams. I still suffered with night terrors as an adult. Eventually, I also started dreaming of attacks on my family while I lay helpless to intervene. Somehow I sensed the horrible things these bad guys intended to do without them verbalizing their threats. I just knew.

In the months leading up to September 2001, my dreams started escalating. I began experiencing strange things that had never before happened in all my years of nightmares. I physically felt and smelled things like carpet fibers against my cheek and the heavy scent of dust. The counselor explained that these were most likely sensory memories coming up. They were a sort of representation of things I had experienced in the past, but only in bits and pieces. Sometimes I could connect a sensation to a particular event from my childhood. Other times I could not. These were the most intriguing. They were like bread crumbs that my subconscious would leave behind trying to lead me to something. The clues seemed vaguely familiar, but my mind struggled to form a concrete memory.

In one particular dream, I felt an evil presence in the room with me. I couldn't move a muscle, and the presence was coming closer. I was terrified. As it began to overtake my body, all I could do was cry out in my mind for God to help me. The presence was a heavy tingling sensation above me that passed into my entire body. It was a definite invasion, but very general all over. Then it retreated back the way it had come. Almost instantly, I felt another gentler presence with me. It invaded me much the same way, but felt comforting and reassuring. It was shocking to wake up from, but my mind began pouring over the details, trying to make sense of it.

After several days of contemplation, the conclusion that I came to was that the first presence was something bad that had happened to me as a child. My conscious just wasn't ready to reveal it fully yet. The second presence I believe without a doubt was the Holy Spirit. I think that He came to protect me in that terrifying moment as a child and that He was the only thing that held me together. In the dream, I sensed that God was telling me that He had to withdraw somewhat to let this evil thing come to the surface but that He would always be near. It was scary. I didn't dare imagine what might be revealed in time. Yet it was reassuring that God was conscious of me and my struggles and that He cared.

On the night of September 10, 2001, I had a nightmare like no other. I again experienced a sensation in my dream state, but it was not vague this time. There was a presence in the room, approaching me. I was lying on my back, unable to move or call for help. Again I sensed a tingling sensation overtaking me. Then I felt it. Two distinct hands holding my legs down. It unlocked a new level of terror deep inside me. When I awoke, I could not shake the eerie feeling. I was numb and hollow inside. The hands felt so real and restricting. Yet there was something odd about their placement. With the events unfolding the morning of September 11, however, there was no time to process or even fully absorb what I'd just personally undergone. The whole nation was in turmoil, and this threat seemed more prominent than my individual one. This "living nightmare" presented its own set of questions and confusion to sort through. My personal horror became mingled with layers of anguish, distress, and disbelief. Any resolution of either matter was merely a faint hope beyond the horizon as I stumbled powerless and fragmented through the days that followed.

CHAPTER 2

My husband and I had just entered our twenties when we got married. Life seemed simpler then. We were very much in love and wanted to spend all of our time together. This was our basis for happiness. In reality, however, we were young, naive, and both carried a lot of emotional baggage into our relationship. The worst thing that either one of us could imagine for the future was the other being unfaithful to our marriage vows. With that line drawn in the sand, so to speak, we blindly set out on our happily ever after.

It didn't take long for the pressures of finishing school, working opposite shifts, and having our first child to start pressing in on us. Our communication skills were surface level at best. The only way serious issues were addressed was through angry outbursts and crying meltdowns. I threw myself into being a mom while still working full-time. My husband felt neglected and easily found a sympathetic ear at work. I saw the signs and tried to talk to him openly. Even that couldn't derail the train wreck to come.

I suspected. He denied. The coworker soon left the business, and things started improving at home. So even though it was hard, I chose to trust my husband and move on. He even started helping me get our daughter ready in the mornings before work. This created a strong bond between the two of them. Up until that time, he had felt left out of the parenting process and sensed that our child didn't know him. This new morning routine dramatically changed all that. Our nine-month-old quickly became daddy's little girl, and she had him wrapped around her little finger. It was a match made in heaven that remains strong to this day.

Three months after putting the suspicion behind us, however, I received a disturbing call from a man I didn't know. It was the former coworker's husband. When the truth came out, I was crushed two times over—once for the infidelity, twice for the months of living a lie. I felt humiliated, betrayed, and worthless. For the first time in my life, I couldn't even pray. It felt like my heart, and my life, were shattered into a million pieces. The only thing that kept me going was our baby girl. She was the one thing that I could still find happiness in, which led to gratitude and hope. After a couple of weeks, I began to realize that God was answering unspoken prayers—things I needed but was too weak to articulate. It was then that I genuinely appreciated the gift of the Holy Spirit interceding for us, as it says in Romans 8:26. Truly amazing.

Of course, there was a lot of heartache and tears during this time, along with anger and combativeness. However, I discovered some important truths through the stages of this tragedy. For one thing, all my self-worth was tied up in my husband. I hadn't realized that he had become a sort of idol in my heart that I unconsciously put before God. There were also a lot of unspoken expectations I had for him that were not realistic. This was my first glimpse into knowing that I had a God-shaped hole in my heart and that I was unfairly trying to make my husband fill it. I was trying to bury all the pain and loneliness of my childhood with our marriage. Looking back now, I can see that it was the equivalent of wrapping a pretty bow around a gaping wound.

There was another more positive truth revealed as well. Naturally, when a relationship crashes and burns, most of us turn to a close friend. Oddly enough, that's when I realized that my husband truly was my best friend. It hit me that first night after receiving the devastating news. The thought of my husband touching me was revolting, but I needed my best friend to hold me. So I laid down the guidelines, and that's what he did. All these years later, we still marvel at the significance of that realization. It is our deep friendship that fuels the love we have for each other to this day. It sparked our relationship, rekindled our broken hearts, and is what keeps the warmth glowing between us. Friendship is the greatest constant through each stage of life that we've faced.

Another equally important revelation for me was that my husband is God's child before anything else. That means their relationship takes precedence over our marriage. I wanted God to keep my husband from hurting me. But He had things He wanted to teach each of us through this experience. Part of it for me was separating my feelings from those of my husband. I needed to find my worth in my Heavenly Father rather than earthly securities like a loving husband. I also needed to find my strength in Him, more than I even knew at the time. For my husband, at least in part, God wanted him to know what a gift our family was and to never doubt how much he wanted it. He later shared with me that being with someone else left him feeling empty. It made him realize that what we had was very special and worth fighting for. I truly believe that all these revelations were a vital foundation for getting us and our marriage through future trials, ones that God knew were on the horizon.

CHAPTER 3

For several years, we continued to seek God's leading in repairing our marriage. That's not to say that we didn't struggle. It always seemed that when one of us wanted to give up, the other was unwilling. Not once were we both ready to throw in the towel at the same time. I believe that was all God. Also we came to a place where things were better, but I struggled to once again give my heart to my husband. We prayed, and God answered. He led us to an intensive marriage weekend that left us drained but gave us new hope. We went on to facilitate two sessions of the course at our home church, while working through the material ourselves. Some who knew us joked that the course must work wonders because we soon became pregnant with our second child.

At some point, I remember thinking that the only thing worse than what our marriage had just survived would be to lose a child. I'm not sure if I was trying to gain perspective or just identifying my new greatest fear. Either way, the phrase "Be careful what you wish for" comes to mind. Although I wasn't making a wish, I most definitely drew a line that, I guess, I unconsciously expected God or life not to cross. After all, I reasoned, one tragedy was enough for a lifetime, right?

None of this was even on my radar as my due date approached. Our oldest, who was four at this time, took ill for a few days. She threw up a couple of times and was otherwise listless for three days. I just figured she had caught a stomach bug at preschool and did all the usual mothering things to ease her misery. Then my husband came down with it. He said it was the worst flu he had ever had. In turn, I became ill as well. My head and neck hurt so severely that all

I could do was sleep. Maybe the dots are already connecting for you, but at the time, we were just focused on getting through. I decided that this was no ordinary flu and agreed that it was the worst illness I had ever experienced.

Just as I was getting better, it was time for a routine pregnancy checkup. My due date was still three weeks out, but my doctor was sure I'd go into labor early. The next day, my water broke. By that evening, we had another healthy, beautiful daughter. After a couple of days, we got to take her home. All was fine at first. She was smiling (I swear) and nursing well. On the fourth day, however, she suddenly became lethargic and wasn't really eating anymore. I was extremely concerned but equally exhausted. Sometime in the night, I said a prayer for God to watch over her because I couldn't keep my eyes open any longer. He did, by the way.

The next morning, our baby was running a slight temperature. I had no idea how much Tylenol a five-day-old could take, so I called the pediatrician. They said to come in because newborns don't usually run a fever. Of course, when time for the appointment came, our baby perked up considerably and even nursed while we were there. With no signs of illness, the doctor sent us on our way. However, as soon as we got back home, she took a turn for the worse. Our baby's tiny six-pound body lay listless in the bassinet. Her breathing was shallow and quick. I called the doctor back, knowing that I sounded like a worrisome first-time mother, but something was seriously wrong. Fortunately, our pediatrician didn't hesitate to have us bring her straight to the neo-natal ICU.

The next forty-eight hours became our new standard of horrifying. An hour after we arrived, these doctors prepared us for the worst. They said that cultures showed our child had bacterial meningitis. Her chance of survival was low. And if she did survive, she'd most likely be in a vegetative state. They just kept saying these things repeatedly until we broke down in sobs of tears. We immediately contacted friends who got the church prayer chain involved. Within an hour, we could feel a palpable sense of support surrounding us. We sat up all of that night in the waiting room, praying and praying until we couldn't repeat our pleas anymore. Then I started singing songs of praise in my mind. It sounds like a strange inclination, I know. But it was something like I was on a long-distance call with heaven that I couldn't hang up. Even though there was no further need for me to keep pleading my case, I still needed to be connected to this literal lifeline. So I did the only other thing that I could think to do in my fearful, exhausted state. I praised the only one truly in control.

Before the sun was even up, a new doctor came on shift. He sat us down for another "preparation speech." Once again we were brought to tears. Completely distraught, I began picturing a tiny baby coffin holding my child instead of me. I couldn't imagine how we could survive losing our baby. I was sure that I didn't have the strength to raise a special-needs child, though, either. Inconsolable, I finally cried out to God in my mind, "This isn't fair! I'm still healing from my last hurt. I can't get through this!" Instantly, I heard a response in my soul. It was something like "Oh really?" Then somehow I just knew that I had to admit that God could indeed get me through this. After all, He had just gotten me through the deepest pain I'd ever experienced and was faithfully rebuilding our marriage. So I relented and admitted with a heavy sigh that very thing. It wasn't enough to simply treat this as a passing thought. I had to make the acknowledgement "out loud" in my head. Thinking back, it was definitely a full-surrender moment. However, remembering Jesus's prayer in the garden, I added, "But if it is at all possible, please don't let our baby die."

Much later on, I came to realize how important it was to acknowledge God's ability to get me through tragedy. It was something that I thought I knew, but I needed to be fully sure of His sovereignty even over my greatest pain and fears. At that moment when I confessed it "out loud" to myself, it became like a declaration set in stone. Much like the alter of stones that God told Moses to build after the parting of the Red Sea so that generations to come would know of His mighty works for them. I'm now so grateful for that moment because it provides a point at which I can go back, regain my courage, renew my strength, and press on without having to pour over all the pain and struggle that it took for me to get there. In other words, it's like a mile marker on my path of life. When I begin to feel lost and overwhelmed, I don't have to go all the way back to start. A certain amount of ground has been covered well enough in the past that I don't have to tread over it again in order to get where I need to be for the next season of my life. It would be a marker that I would have to go back to many times in the years to come. It always provides me hope when I need it most to carry on.

Unknown to me, at that same time, my husband had a similar experience in his spirit too. Then within that very same hour, the doctor stuck his head in through the waiting room doorway and said that he needed to speak with us right away. Gravely numb by this point, we couldn't imagine what more he would have to tell us. That's when a miracle occurred! The doctor informed us that the cultures in the lab were not growing bacteria as expected. You see, once the initial sample confirms bacteria, it takes a couple days of incubation time to determine exactly what strain of bacteria is present. Treatment began immediately with what they called an antibiotic cocktail until lab results narrowed down which medicine would best fight the specific bacteria causing our daughter's illness. However (I like to think of it as a Hallelujah *however*), a recheck of her lab work showed that our child's meningitis was viral, not bacterial. The doctor figured the original sample must have been contaminated somehow. We knew differently. It was a miracle in answer to our prayers.

CHAPTER 4

O ur daughter illness was still very serious. The doctor said she had a fifty-fifty chance of survival. The good news was that we had brought her in quickly. Treatment continued, but they no longer anticipated any permanent damage to her brain or spine. A tremendous weight was lifted from us and our numbness faded to hope. The healing process progressed quickly from there. After a couple of days, our baby was transferred out of NICU to the pediatric floor. By the end of the week, we were able to return home with her. This was tremendous considering the original estimated time of care was predicted to be as much as four months. Once our household settled down again, I realized a horrible truth. Our four-year-old had suffered from meningitis and we had no clue! We could have lost her as well. I am so very grateful that God was attentive and watching over us even when we didn't have the sense to know how badly we were in need of His care. Thank you, Heavenly King and Father!

Life continued with all its joys and stresses. Eventually, we talked about having another baby. Our plan was to start trying to get pregnant in August of the following year because by then our girls would be ages six and two years. Perfect timing in our estimation, but not God's. While visiting my in-laws fourteen hours away, I started feeling nauseous and suspiciously tired. The plan for the trip back home was to share driving at night so the girls would sleep through most of it. Only thirty minutes into our return, I started vomiting. My poor husband. It was all I could do to clean myself up between episodes and hope for blessed unconsciousness. He had to drive the whole way home, which ended up being a lot longer than fourteen hours. It was one of those experiences—you know, the kind we can only hope we will be able to look back on and laugh about…someday.

Eventually, I decided that God must have a purpose for this unplanned timing. When we later found out that we were having a boy, I was sure He was blessing us. I recalled the words of Isaiah 55:8: "For my thoughts are not your thoughts, neither are your ways my ways, declares the LORD. As the heavens are higher than the earth, so are my ways higher than your ways and my thoughts higher than your thoughts." I was also reminded of the wisdom shared in Proverbs 16:9: "In his heart a man plans his course, but the LORD determines his steps." Growing up in the church, I knew these verses well. I just never imagined the deeply personal way they would come to touch my individual life.

In God's perfect timing, our son was born three days before our oldest daughter started first grade. Just a month earlier, our younger daughter had turned two. Again life was hectic but happy. I would look at my son and think, *I love you so much.* It wasn't too long, though, until that sweet thought began triggering another not-so-good thought: *But you're going to be a good one, right?* Even at that time, I realized this was a lot of pressure for a three-month-old. However, I could not separate the two. They evolved into one cohesive conflicting thought. Apparently, having a son had brought to the surface some unresolved fears in me. What I didn't realize at the time was how significant the age and grade level of our first daughter actually was. This turned out to be an even greater catalyst to impending events. I just wouldn't know it until much later.

It was around that same time that I began struggling with disturbing thoughts and the increasing nightmares. Most of my life had been riddled with scary dreams, but this was a definite escalation of intensity and frequency. Like I alluded to earlier, throughout my teenage years, I'd considered suicide or just wanting to be dead. I had specific thoughts about driving off the side of the road. The justification in my mind was "I'll show them" or "At least nobody could hurt me anymore." It most commonly occurred along a particular stretch of curvy, potentially treacherous road that I drove back and forth on for work. With the whole "Thou shalt not murder" thing and my ambiguous clarification of where suicide fell into that mix, though, death didn't seem like a viable option. Even though I was excruciatingly miserable in life, I wanted relief, not eternal damnation, so I endured.

Although these particular thoughts had not been a problem for many years, they once again started plaguing me. There was a section of bridge crossing over a busy highway near our house. I drove over it several times a week since my daughter's preschool was just on the other side from our house. Every time I approached that spot the thought would unconsciously pop up to plummet over the edge into the traffic below. It was the same depressive urge from my teen years, only now it was happening with my children in the car. I would usually reason with myself that I would never want to hurt my kids and keep on driving. But the persistence of this impulse was disturbing, and I wondered at what point I might not be able to resist it anymore. I was also puzzled as to why this impulse had resurfaced now.

Thankfully, I knew where to go with my serious concerns. Because of our previous marital problems, I already had a counselor, whom I trusted and felt comfortable opening up with. I know that if this relationship had not already been in place, I would not have sought help. It was such an overwhelming time that I would have just kept pushing through aimlessly until something snapped. I am so grateful to God for arranging the right circumstances to be in place when I needed them most. He knew all along what was coming, and even though I didn't appreciate it at the time, He had been guiding me all of the way.

Upon my first visit back to the counseling office, the therapist quietly listened as I told him what I had been feeling. Then he said four concise little words: "Are you ready now?" I had forgotten about our previous, although brief, conversation on the subject of possible childhood trauma. Over the past six years in and out of counseling, he had never pushed me to focus on this avenue of my life. Maybe it was wise patience or because I certainly had enough present-day issues to focus on. Nonetheless, I realized in a single moment how long he had let this concept sit on the back burner until the time was right. By nature I am a "picker"—you know, the kind that pops a pimple and picks at a scab. I can't leave things alone. So this level of fortitude is mind boggling for me.

So I was doubly blessed to have both a wise, patient counselor who respectfully trusted God's timing and an omnipotent, merciful Father God who, knowing what needed to unfold, protected me for a time and prepared me for what was to come. I'm actually in awe of how patient both God and our counselor were with me considering my unappreciative attitude much of time. I now realize without a doubt that if God had not strengthened me through the two previous trials of my marriage and our daughter's illness, I would not have survived this third one of having my past resurface. This season would require a more grounded perspective and an unwavering resolve that God could be trusted with my greatest fears.

When our marriage problems surfaced, I thought my life was over. What I learned was that only God can fill the void inside of me and that He actively guides me day by day. Almost losing our second child didn't seem survivable. However, God most clearly reminded me that through His strength I could go on and deeply cemented this truth in my heart. Of course, this enlightenment came much later on. At the time, I was on the verge of disintegration. What I didn't realize at the time was that this depth of knowing that truth would be a necessary anchor for choppier seas than I could even fathom which were just on the horizon. In other words, it was a holy "Buckle up, child! A storm to beat all previous storms is coming for you." Thank You so much, Daddy, for caring and for carrying me safely through.

CHAPTER 5

When my counselor asked me if I was ready now, my answer was emphatically, "I have to know." And that's how I felt, like I had little choice in the matter. There was no amount of will that could stop the things that were happening to me. I began having very unique experiences. Dreams of sorts, but somehow quite real. One of the most distinct occurred while lying down with my two-year-old for an afternoon nap. It began with feeling the mattress moving like someone, or something, was climbing into the bed with us. Somewhat consciously, I thought about making sure that my daughter wasn't being harmed. Physically, however, I was laid out flat on my back, completely immobilized. Then I became aware of something overtaking my body. My best description is of a large tingling sensation hovering over me. The sensation proceeded to press down onto and then into my whole body. Although panicked, I remained incapacitated, powerless to resist or even open my eyes. All I could manage to do was cry out in my mind for Jesus to help me. The sensation withdrew back the same way that it had come. Almost immediately, I felt another less threatening sensation overcome my body in a similar way. It was distinctly lighter and less scary. It lingered briefly then retreated as well.

Upon sharing this encounter with my therapist, he asked if I had felt specific pressure anywhere in particular on my body. For years, I had been combatting dreams in which I was unable to move or react. But I never felt specifically pinned down at any one point like my shoulders or arms. This experience was quite different, though. It was more distinct than my previous dreams yet still without exact pressure points. Over several weeks of processing the event, my best discernment was as follows. The first large overall sensation was most certainly an intrusion upon my person. I felt defenseless and frozen in fear. The second lighter presence was God's Spirit letting me know that He was with me. Sometime later, I decided that God was telling me, without words, that He had to back off in order to allow this evil to unfold but that He would still be near. I know that, at first, this doesn't sound right. However, I looked at it this way. God cannot abide where evil is. In order for me to purge whatever this was that was haunting me, it had to come forth in my consciousness. So God was making room for that to happen by letting me experience these things yet would most assuredly still watch over me through it.

A couple of years later, while rethinking over this event, I feel like I received further clarification from God. I had always believed that I had received the Holy Spirit at the moment of my baptism at age nine. It was because I felt this tremendous, overwhelming sensation of light and joy flow through my chest as I was raised from the water. I just thought that was how everyone felt in that moment. Over the years, however, it became obvious that not everybody could relate. For the first time now, I connected that experience at my baptism with the lighter, comforting sensation of my more recent experience. They were strikingly similar, even the same in nature. In that very moment I came to believe that it was at my greatest hour of need (as an innocent, helpless child being violated) that God bestowed His Spirit on me. Although I was unaware, it was the Holy Spirit that had held me together in my fragile state until the time was right to process it fully. How else can I explain twenty-plus years of artfully keeping such a secret from myself? It boggles my mind and is beyond understanding except that I lived it. Not only that, but now I've been delivered from that dark weight of it. I'll address this more in a later part of my story.

Before I lose some of my readers here, let me cite a verse out of scripture for you. Romans 8:26–27 says, "The Spirit helps us in our weakness. We do not know what we ought to pray for, but the Spirit Himself intercedes for us with groans that words cannot express. And He who searches our hearts knows the mind of the Spirit, because the Spirit intercedes for the saints in accordance with God's will."

Oh my goodness, I could quote the whole chapter; it's so exciting! If you want to be uplifted, I encourage you to read it on your own. Right now even. I'll hold your place. To keep on point, however, I'll just mention two more things. Verse 31 proclaims, "If God is for us, who can be against us?" And verse 34 reminds us, "Christ Jesus, who died—more than that, who was raised to life—is at the right hand of God and is also interceding for us." I hope that you can understand and excuse my personal enthusiasm. But isn't that what the scriptures are supposed to do—speak personally to us? For now, what I believe about my baptism is that the overwhelming sensation in my chest was the Holy Spirit, already residing in me, leaping for joy at my public display of choosing Jesus as my Savior. I've only felt that same chest sensation a handful of other times in my life. Each and every time was when I would concentrate and try to even begin to imagine the reality of what being in heaven will be like someday. To quote a song, "Yes, it overwhelms and satisfies my soul!" ("One Thing Remains" by Jesus Culture).

Some of the other unique experiences that I encountered during this time were smells and physical movement in my dream state. Two smells in particular were cigarette smoke and heavy dust within a carpet. Both occurred while hiding from bad people coming to hurt me. This was another point that my therapist questioned me about. How did I know what these imagined intruders' intentions were? My only answer was that I just knew. It was all very generic; however, the smells seem to be distinctively connected to my fear since they were new and quite realistic. There was also a period of time that extreme fear plagued my sleep. I would be dreaming of my room and myself in the present time, except something would begin dragging me off the bed. Again, there was no exact placement of physical contact anywhere on my body. It was from the direction of my feet, but I never knew what exactly was pulling. I absolutely did know, however, that it was evil (like the fire and brimstone kind) and was sure that if it succeeded in pulling me completely off the bed, I would not come back. Terrified is what I was, beyond anything I had ever experienced. The only way I could sleep was with the very real physical assurance of my husband's arms around me with his promise that he would not let me go. It was just a dream, but it felt intensely real.

Then it finally happened. On the eve of 9-11, I had an experience in which I distinctly felt someone touching me. Sometime in the night, our two-year-old had gotten up and turned on all the lights in the house before climbing into our bed. My husband turned off the lights while I took our daughter back to her bottom bunk in our girls' room. She curled up in the top right corner just above my left shoulder. I sprawled out toward the lower half of the bed and drifted back to sleep. Once again, I ended up in the vulnerable position of lying on my back when suddenly I was startled by hands pressing down on my shins. It was a somewhat numb, tingling feeling, but were distinctly hands. I was overcome with terror and a little hysterical. At this point, I thought that I had awoken, so what comes next felt very real, although I was still dreaming.

I jolted up and seized a shadowy figure by his collar. I looked squarely into his face but didn't recognize him. He looked almost not human with this blank, eerie stare to his eyes. It was like he was looking right through me. I thought to myself that he must be hurting my daughter. That's why she was disturbed in the night. I said something like, "I need to kill you!" And I meant it! But the ghostly man slipped out of my grasp and retreated under the bed, wearing a sinister grin. I again grabbed his shoulders and pulled his torso back up. I had him pinned backward over the side of the mattress, desperately trying to figure out how to destroy him. I realized, however, that I couldn't do it. I couldn't murder someone. Just then my husband walked into the room. I yelled for him to kill this guy. He flatly replied "Do it yourself" and suggested using a pen to stab him with. (Do you see the irony here? Or maybe it was divine foretelling!) Nevertheless, I couldn't do it.

Then I "woke up" again like from a dream, but I was actually still asleep. I felt horrified and began crying uncontrollably. I got out of bed and headed across the hall to seek comfort from my spouse. As I stepped through the doorway, however, I saw my parents in our living room. My dad didn't acknowledge me, but seeing him made me suck back my emotions. My mom looked at me and said that they had been waiting for us to wake up to visit. With that, I sucked back my emotions even more. By the time I reached my husband, they were all chatting, paying no attention to me. So I decided to get my notebook from the other side of the room to write this event down.

That's when I heard my therapist's voice behind me. When I turned around, I saw a little girl standing beside him. I didn't recognize her, but she was about the same age as our oldest daughter, about first or second grade. No one else seemed to see or hear them. My therapist was singing an eerie tune with music like from a wind-up box. The words were something like "Come out of the shadows." I couldn't remember them exactly when I did wake up. Overall, the message was about letting go and recalling what I needed to remember. It was all rather creepy in itself. I don't think I even ever told my counselor about the song. Reading back on my journaling from that experience, a lot of the imagery makes sense now. At that time, however, it was almost too much to take in.

As I continued approaching my notebook, the closer I got the less I could feel the emotions. I sensed control taking over, like a wall was building back up. By the time I really did awake, my emotions were stuffed way down. The transition from terror and hysterics to an almost detached state was both abrupt and surreal. Conveying my dream to my husband was difficult because my emotions felt so distant and out of touch. I was left extremely anxious, trembling inside. And that was how I began my morning on September 11, 2001, before any of that day's horrible events even took place.

CHAPTER 6

Six months of weekly sessions with my counselor was keeping me sane, but it hadn't produced any answers as to why I was going through this season of heightened anxiety. Having someone safe to tell about all my strange experiences and feelings was therapeutic. I had also started medicine to help my nerves. I even tried methods of self-meditation with little success. It was at this point that my counselor referred me to a psychologist specializing in image therapy.

I was extremely nervous about opening up to a stranger, but I was desperate for progress. During my first visit, I sat in a recliner, trying to calm my nerves by wrapping my arms tightly around my stomach. This was a familiar comforting technique from my childhood. In my teen years, I came to realize that this was a response to chaos. My anxiety would escalate to the point that I felt like, if I didn't physically hold myself together, I would shatter into a million pieces. Sitting in this new office across from an unfamiliar, all be it friendly, face I also thought of my stance as a somewhat protective barrier around me. On top of all of this, I then had to close my eyes and try to relax in a reclined position with my feet up. Talk about feeling vulnerable.

My first task upon starting image therapy was to picture a safe place in my mind. Some suggestions were a secluded beach or an open meadow. My immediate response was panic, my reasoning being that anyone could come running into those places at any moment. They weren't guarded or protected in any way. The only image that I could come up with that truly felt safe was a barren white tile floor, something like a hospital would have, surrounded on all sides by clouds.

It was sterile and empty but bright and well protected. There was a celestial feel, definitely not of this earth. Therefore, it was safe from any possible intrusion or trespass. At the time, I was scrambling to imagine somewhere that I could feel completely safe. Now, looking back, I can see that there simply was no place that already existed that felt impenetrable. Also, being surrounded by clouds seems to connect to being covered by God's love and protection. Being alone there didn't bother me. Somehow I didn't feel lonely, just at peace.

The next task was to think back to a prominent memory from my childhood. Consciously, I knew that I had almost no memories of first grade. I could remember times in my life as far back as pre-school, but nearly nothing for that one-year span. I figured that was where we needed to start or somewhere before, but something told me to picture myself in second grade. The psychologist encouraged me to follow my instincts. So I replayed a memory of building up some blocks in the classroom with some of my classmates. For some reason, we were having inside recess. We just chatted away as we built.

At first, it was as if I were part of the scene, seeing it all through my own eyes as a memory. Then my perspective seamlessly shifted to where my adult self was watching my seven-year-old self from a few feet away. I appeared to be having fun, without a care in the world. That's exactly how I remembered it. This little girl didn't seem to need anything from me. She looked well-adjusted, healthy, and happy on the outside. However, it would turn out that I would learn something new about myself from her before we were done.

At the psychologist's suggestion, I imagined my adult self speaking to the younger me. I said hello and introduced myself. This didn't seem weird to her at all. Our interaction was quite pleasant and friendly as a matter of fact. I don't recall much of what was actually said. I just remember that she was full of wonder and joy like any small child. I do know that I felt love and compassion for her much like a mother and child. This was probably a significant, although unconscious, shift from the self-hate I felt most of my life. It would certainly allow me to extend, and in turn receive, grace later on. As my session came to an end, I had to say goodbye to my younger self.

I promised to be back soon, though, for another visit. So I left her there contently playing until my return.

Consciously, it seemed like silly pretending. Yet somehow each scene played out intuitively. Even the interactions, which weren't actual memories at all, flowed effortlessly. Although I didn't know my younger self's exact thoughts or feelings, there was an instant connection between us. Something indescribable but also undeniable. I believe it was an unwitting reconnection with a part of myself tucked away and forgotten as life moved on. But this time, I could be the missing equation that was lacking before. I could be the adult caretaker of my younger self and extend much needed empathy, love, and understanding. In a sense, I could now be the hero of my own story, but that spot of honor is actually reserved for God. Yet He would use me in an important role play to unlock years of neglectful pain and replace it with healing peace.

During our next visit, I asked my second-grade self if she wanted to come and see my safe place. She liked its serenity, but there wasn't much to do, of course. Somehow we began blowing bubbles. They got bigger and bigger until one became like a carnival ride. We sat inside of it, able to see all around. There was only sky and clouds surrounding us as we floated upward. Then we saw two very large hands gently scoop us up in our bubble. There was no question that these hands belonged to God. They neither scared nor confused us. It was more of a sweet, unexpected gesture from a heavenly being we both already knew and trusted. We looked at each other with wide-open eyes and smiled. A gentle breeze from behind sent us off sailing across the sky. We laughed and wondered at the thrill of it all.

At some point, I asked the young girl if everything was good in her life. Without a word, she glanced downward, turning her face away. The smile on her face quickly melted to a frown. For the first time since we'd met, I could tell there was something greatly upsetting her. Until that moment, there had been no sign of sadness or pain. It was then that I understood she was holding a terrible secret inside. I now knew there was more to uncover. I realized that behind her carefree facade was a wound too severe to see the light of day. I wondered how long this small child had been carrying such a heavy burden. My heart went out to her. I didn't push for details. I simply asked if she wanted to spend more time together on my next visit. She did. So we said goodbye until then.

I'm not exactly sure where she "stayed." We didn't return to the second-grade classroom. Not because it wasn't safe or pleasant. Maybe it was because we had made a special and much needed, even vital connection in that moment. I needed to realize that this young girl did need something from me. She needed to know someone truly cared about her. What I do know is that she was my constant companion every visit after that. Every time I returned to my safe place, she met me there. I don't even think she ever said another word. Her face was just always welcoming, and she was right by my side the whole time I was there in my mind.

CHAPTER 7

Naturally, the next place in time to visit in my mind was my first-grade year. Since it was confirmed that something was bothering me by the age of seven, I needed to dig deeper into my past. I was nervous going there but determined to give the younger version of myself what she needed from me. So I asked the second grader if she wanted to come with me. Without hesitation, she eagerly nodded yes and took hold of my hand. Again, I don't know exactly how we "traveled" to that classroom. It was off to the right or east of my safe place. There was a definite dividing expanse between the two locations. I just remember picturing the room best I could from memory, and there we were.

From my vantage point, the room was rectangular from left to right. The long wall across from me was made of concrete blocks halfway up with a row of windows extending the whole length of the room. Outside was a grassy area, and across that was another identically shaped classroom of older students. Our school had a long main hallway with four or five wings of classrooms to one side. Each wing typically housed one grade level and an additional room for special classes, like music, art, or library that served all grades. In between each of these wings was a small strip of grass that was never really utilized for any purpose. If you stood at the windows, you could look across into the other classrooms. Generally, we were trained not to pay attention to the view. And of course, at that grade level, a lot of artwork, science projects, and such hung on the majority of the glass. Also our class was made up of six-year-olds sitting at tiny desks, so I don't think any of us could see above the block portion of the wall anyway.

The front of the classroom was to the far right of the space and simply contained two chalkboards. I know this to be correct because I have two brief memories of first grade. One was during a Halloween party. Our class was divided into two or three teams and given the task of drawing a witch on the board. I think this memory stands out so clearly for two reasons. First, because we kids were never allowed to write on the chalkboards, so it was an exciting privilege. Secondly, I had a very specific vision in my mind of what the witch would look like. Each child got a turn to draw only one part of the picture and then the combined efforts were compared. I was one of the first to draw my portion, then stood back to watch the rest add their parts. It hadn't occurred to me in my excitement that my classmates would have different pictures in their minds. So when the end result turned out completely differently than I had hoped, it made me stop and ponder. I don't know why it was so significant. Maybe it was a coming-of-age moment when self-focus began emerging into other awareness. It probably only lasted two minutes, but I can still recall the whole event with vivid detail. For some reason, that brief activity left a lasting impression on me that superseded the mental block within which my mind had otherwise entrapped the whole of my first-grade experience.

My only other memory of that year stands out for a much different reason. I recall sitting somewhere midway in the rows of seating which faced the chalkboards with the wall of windows to the left. The teacher's desk was tucked in the back corner of the room parallel to the rows of desks. I raised my hand to ask a question about the assignment that we were all working on quietly at or seats. When the teacher leaned in to answer, all I could pay attention to was her extremely strong cigarette-smoke breath. I remember trying not to breathe while she spoke and nodding that I understood without any eye contact. I was so affected by the smell that I hadn't heard a word she said. The only thing I learned in that moment was to never ask the teacher a question again. And I very much doubt that I ever did.

Obviously, I can place the chalkboard memory in the month of October since it was Halloween. The bad breath memory I'm not so sure about. However, I believe it was early in the year for several reasons. I vaguely recall green grass outside through the windows and wearing clothes suitable for warm weather. Also it seems like one of my first encounters with this teacher because I wasn't hesitant to raise my hand but vowed never to make that mistake again. I've always thought it very strange that I have numerous detailed memories of preschool and kindergarten but almost nothing of first grade—nothing of classmates, recess, friendships, interests…nothing. The only other details I could recall were my teacher's name, that she had very shortly cut brown hair (almost boy-like), and that she knew my mom was a teacher at the high school in our district. During image therapy, I also recalled that she always wore pants, not skirts or dresses. That detail seemed to become significant during a subsequent interaction with my first-grade self. I'll revisit that later in my story.

The majority of my following sessions were focused on visiting that first-grade classroom. That's why I wanted you to be able to envision it with as much detail as possible. As I mentioned, the teacher's desk was situated in the rear far corner of the room with her back to the windows. Her desk overlooked a large area rug on the floor just behind the rows of student desks. I only had a formless sense of the very back portion of the room. It loomed dark and shadowy off to the left of my full-range vantage point. Unfortunately, it was directly between there and my safe place. From the very first visit, I was leery of the space. When it came time to end the session, I was paralyzed with fear of crossing through the area to return to my sanctuary on the other side. That was where we ended every visit. I suppose it was to calm the anxieties that surfaced from peering into the past. Giving me a safe place to transition from there back to reality allowed me to put the progress on hold without fully carrying the weight of it all through the coming week. It was an ingenious, very necessary coping mechanism looking back.

I really had no idea why that space was so ill-defined yet terrifying. Now I realize that it stemmed from the deepest, darkest secret within me. I would come to find out that it was the very spot of an unspeakable horror I faced as a child. For now, however, I still wasn't ready to face it. Simply returning to the room took all the courage I could muster. I needed rescuing. This was one of the very few times that my psychologist interjected a suggestion. He offered up the idea of a vehicle or a bridge to cross over the gap. Again, one thing came to my mind that was the only acceptable solution for me. I call it the "pope mobile". Essentially, it was a large clear bubble with motorized wheels (a lot like the carnival-ride bubble that I described earlier, now that I think about it).

At some point, growing up, I remember seeing a news report about the pope visiting somewhere. I was neither Catholic nor a grown-up, so the details escaped me. What caught my attention, though, was the pope riding in a procession of cars with one strange modification to his personal vehicle. He was waving to the crowds from within a large plastic dome-shaped bulletproof shield. I'm pretty sure the contraption was fashioned to protect the pope from a threat of assassination. The scene was certainly unique and a little humorous, so it stuck with me. In any event, that was the mode of transportation that I chose. I felt cocooned with impenetrable safety, sitting inside that thing. It kind of made me laugh at myself a bit too. This became the preferred mode of transportation from here on out.

CHAPTER 8

Communication with my first-grade self didn't come as easily as it had with my second grader. She was always sitting quietly at her desk face down. Her posture was very tense, as if she were hunched over guarding her personal space. Come to think of it, maybe it was her heart she was protecting or tightly trying to hold it together. When I came to another impasse, the psychologist told me that sometimes it helped to distance one's self further in imagery by picturing a television or movie screen. He said this could help me feel safer to explore for more details. So I imagined a small television set at the corner of the first grader's school desk. Upon doing this, my vantage point automatically zoomed in closer to the child to see what she was looking at. All I could see on the screen were some buttons on a sweater. Hands were undoing the buttons one by one. It really didn't mean anything to me or seem to shed any light on what was troubling the child. Then it happened. My vantage point began to pan out wide again. For the first time, the little girl turned her face toward me. Our eyes locked. And with a terrified look on her face, she mouthed two words: "Help me!"

At that point, I sucked in a breath and began sobbing uncontrollably. This took the psychologist by surprise. I know because it was the one and only time that his voice elevated above its usual calm, peaceful tone. He frantically asked me what had happened. As I told him, the first grader's attention turned back toward her desk with the same rigid frame as before. To this day, that face of horror is the most disturbing thing I've ever seen. Yes, it was scary to see that amount of terror in a small girl's eyes. However, I think it was the unseen connection that existed between the most vulnerable part of me and the damaged innocence of my six-year-old self that allowed the fear and pain to flow so sudden and intensely.

That was definitely a turning point in our visits. I had new resolve to figure out what was going on deep inside of me. That little girl needed an advocate, someone to uncover her secret and release her from the eternal hell she was trapped inside. It didn't happen quickly, though. The first-grade me still didn't open up and talk. However, she did venture to leave her desk. Neither of us could bring ourselves to go to the dark shadows of the back of the classroom yet. This was even the case when I traveled to visit my former elementary school outside of our sessions. I nervously entered the building and proceeded to tour the halls in the exact opposite direction that I knew I needed to go. Saving the dreaded space for last, all I could do was look in through the doorway. Interestingly enough, the very wall shadowed in my mind had since been demolished to expand for a larger library. So there was nothing concrete to see or gain from this adventure. But I do think it was an important step in facing my past and a little poetic justice that the spot had been cleared out and made into something new (not that I appreciated it at the time).

Because we were stalled in progress, the psychologist suggested that we explore the home I grew up in to see if that produced anything. Traveling in our protective bubble, my first-grade self and I went through the house room by room. There was no one home and no furniture or belongings, just a simple layout that I described to the doctor. Nothing there appeared to trigger any emotions in either myself or the little girl. So we decided to leave the safety of our bubble. It didn't feel scary or stressful. However, the first grader didn't say a word or make much eye contact. Again the psychologist made a simple suggestion of letting her draw a picture to help distance ourselves from whatever was holding her communication back. I proceeded to imagine some crayons and a blank piece of paper. Of course, she was eager to color, even a little happy. So I just stood back to observe.

Surprisingly, she drew a bright-red school house to the right side of the sheet. She scribbled some green grass across the bottom of the page. The scene had a cheery feel. In the middle of the paper, she drew a woman with long flowing hair, a smiling face, and a brightly colored dress. If you remember, these are the exact opposite attributes than those of my first-grade teacher. She had a much manlier appearance. Not thinking much about it, though, I asked my younger self if the woman in the picture was a teacher. Without a word, her demeanor changed. She began scribbling furiously over the woman then the whole scene with red and orange crayons. As the colors expanded across the page, they turned to fire. Leaving the drawing behind, we used the bubble mobile to return to the classroom. As she always did, the little girl sat back down at her desk and resumed her guarded stance. I hated leaving her there at the end of our visits each time. But it seemed that was where she needed to stay for the time being. All else remained still around her. The other students and teacher dutifully sat at their own desks, not paying attention to our comings and goings. Therefore, she seemed safe enough.

I'm not exactly sure how many weeks we continued meeting this way. On the one hand, the progress seemed to be moving at a snail's pace. However, each little step drained nearly all my energy physically and mentally. Most of our interactions sound simplistic on paper, maybe even pointless. But each session left me exhausted as if I had run an emotional marathon. I was so set on finding out what was going on inside me that I pushed through two sessions a week for that second six-month period. First, I would visit the psychologist. Then I would process all that had happened by regurgitating every detail with my counselor. I struggled the rest of each week barely able to care for my three young children.

Remember that I mentioned my son was born three days before my oldest daughter began first grade? And our second daughter was only two years old at the time. Oh, and we bought a new house. So by the time I started image therapy, I still had two little ones at home all day. Just the thought of what to make for dinner overwhelmed me to the point of tears. Seriously. I slept whenever possible. Fortunately, nap time was still a part of our daily routine. As much as I hate the analogy, I was like the walking dead. I was a physical and emotional zombie—without the brain eating, of course. (Ha! That would have made meal planning easier, I guess.)

In all seriousness, I was in the worst state of my life. It's really a wonder how my kids and my marriage survived it, let alone me. As bad as it was, though, God had made a way. He knew how hard getting through this necessary purging was going to be. That's why He had started preparing me to endure this exact burden through the other two trials that I mentioned earlier. Remember? As difficult as those ordeals were, they didn't even begin to reach the turmoil of this one. As a matter of fact, it was after weathering this third trial that the full realization hit me.

While lying in bed, saying my nightly prayers, I thanked God for the previous trials that He had used to strengthen and prepare me for the unknown. What! My thoughts stopped dead in their tracks, and I asked myself, "Did I just say that?" Then I recognized that, yes, I was wholeheartedly grateful for the struggles I had to endure. It sounds crazy, I know. I had even told the counselor early on that I would never be thankful for the pain and heartache that brought us there. But I'm telling you, I absolutely would not have survived the process of recalling these repressed memories otherwise. I would not! So I lay there, astonished, facing the ceiling in complete darkness unable to hold back the biggest silly grin my face could muster. I was smiling for my Heavenly Father and no one else. I know it was the Holy Spirit tugging on my shirt tail and essentially saying, "See what I did there? You're welcome, love." Father God, You are amazing!

CHAPTER 9

Several weeks were spent revisiting that first-grade classroom. Each time the interaction was just between myself now and my younger self then. No one else ever bothered us or even seemed to notice us for that matter. It wasn't exactly like they were frozen in time. Nor did any of them walk around the room. We were just free to move and visit without interruption. However, there was still that obscure blackened space at the back of the room. We were both petrified to explore there. I could make out enough to know there was a rectangular carpet on the floor positioned in front of the teacher's desk, but behind the student's rows of chairs. Presumably, there was a back wall beyond the carpet maybe containing some shelves of books or toys. It was unclear, though, because the darkness engulfed the room midway of the carpet.

It was during this portion of therapy that I took that trip back home I mentioned in the last chapter. My psychologist had suggested trying to tour my former elementary school to develop a clearer view of the classroom. I arranged for my mother to accompany me for support. When we arrived at the school, it was empty. There was just a secretary on staff who showed us around. Naturally, it was a lot smaller than I remembered it. Not much had changed. The layout was the same except the halls held different grade levels. The first corridor to the right of the building's entrance no longer housed the first graders as it had when I attended there years before. Still unconsciously but very distinctly, I chose to reminisce in a roundabout pattern that left this hallway for last.

With great trepidation, we finally headed down the long passageway toward my former classroom. We came to the door which was locked. So I peered through the narrow window above the doorknob. The room and the windows were the same, but not its contents. It turned out that this area had been converted to house a larger school library by knocking down the very wall that I was so deathly afraid of and expanding into the room next door. As for visual confirmation, this was a dead end. However, just revisiting this hallowed place was in itself a victory. It may have been this little triumph of facing my fears, in fact, which got me past the block I was experiencing in image therapy. That in combination with my heartbreaking concern for this fragile first grader that I'd come to know.

Even though I was essentially imagining conversing with my former self, the experience was more like my adult self having compassion for say one of my own children. Somehow the role play allowed me to access the deep searing pain locked within me while, at the same time, playing the part of advocate for my former child self. In effect, I was addressing two necessities at the same time. The first was meeting the overlooked needs of a wounded child. Second, was uncovering the secrets that were currently eating me alive. I was being given the chance to rescue myself. In order to do so, however, I would have to determine the details of what actually happened to me way back then. That meant venturing forth into the shadows of the back of that classroom.

Without being too graphic, I'll do my best to explain. I don't remember how the shift in focus occurred, but one session, I was transported back in time, watching events unfold through the eyes of my first-grade self. The recess bell had just rung. For the first time, all of my classmates left their seats and exited the room. The teacher asked me to stay behind, though. I felt disappointed about missing recess and anxious about what she wanted me for. Then she invited me to join her on the carpet to play a board game. I was very hesitant, but she kept talking about the game as she set it up and how much fun it would be to play. So I cautiously approached. The whole time this scene was playing out, I struggled to continue. I would describe the event one sentence at a time like I am here. Then between each line I would say something like "I don't know what else." Each time the psychologist would simply reply, "Just take a deep breath and see what happens." That is it. He never gave me any more direction than that. So bit by bit, I let the memory unfold.

In short, the teacher molested me while gratifying herself. I remember feeling bewildered. There was a look of great pleasure on her face that I couldn't understand as a six-year-old. She didn't even seem to be concerned about what I might be feeling. This is my earliest memory of feeling like an object instead of a human being. At the height of my greatest confusion and fear, I was shown that my instincts and emotions didn't matter. What made it worse was that when the kids started returning from recess, the teacher just got up and walked back to her desk. I was left there in shock, trying to figure out what had just happened while the world went on without even noticing me. I looked to the teacher for some acknowledgement of what had just occurred. She just sat there, doing paperwork. It was like I was invisible.

It is strange how easily a person can be made to question their own sense of reality. Almost immediately, I began to wonder if that really just happened. Not that I even knew what it was that actually took place. I did, however, have a definite sense of violation. But no one else seemed to notice, not even my perpetrator. That was the most confusing part—watching her act like nothing strange had taken place. This was my caretaker seven hours a day, five days a week. She was someone I was supposed to be able to trust and go to for help, and she showed no concern or remorse. I'm sure this internal questioning of my own sanity went on for weeks. It may have been why I never told anyone. Maybe if a caring adult had come to scoop me up in that very moment, I would have confided in them. I don't know for sure. What I did know without a doubt at this point was that something had traumatized me at a young age. Although unbelievable, this eerily seemed to fit.

What I mean by that is, if my life were a puzzle, there was always an elusive sense of a piece missing. That one section that made all the other pieces come together. When I thought back over my childhood, I could remember a lot of inappropriate encounters— so many, in fact, that I wondered why I attracted such unwanted attention. My best friend's older brother and another neighbor boy were a couple of my earliest memories of uncomfortable experiences.

There was a whole string of guys throughout my teen years who made unsolicited advances towards me. Males from school, church, family friends all seemed to have one thing on their mind around me and were eager to see what might happen when they could get me alone. I really adapted to navigating away from these unwelcomed remarks and propositions. Mostly I walked away and ignored them. I just never understood why they kept presenting themselves to me. No boys ever asked me out on a real date. The ones that I liked never liked me back. There were so many confusing signals attacking my self-esteem and sense of security.

All these incidents were indeed unfortunate, but they never quite added up to the amount of emotional turmoil I felt inside. There was always an inexplicit deeper sense of fear and sadness. I often felt more emotion and paranoia than situations truly called for. Of course, I didn't know that my experience was any different from what others felt, but there is no shortage of society picking at people's shortcomings. I was labeled early on as too emotional and scolded for being overly sensitive. Mostly it just felt unfair and like I was on my own. At times, though, even I questioned my own sanity. I wondered what was wrong with me and why God would make me so messed up. So when I say that the culmination of my image therapy just seemed to fit, I mean that there was now an explanation for why I had always felt the way I did.

And wouldn't you know, I had good reason for feeling that way! Who could blame me? As a matter of fact, in light of this new information, I deserve some credit for surviving my childhood. In an ironic twist, the weakness that I had always struggled with turned out to actually be a divine strength bearing weight beyond imagination. Of course, that kind of courageous might could only have come from one place, God. "For I can do all things through Him who gives me strength" (Philippians 4:13). In 2 Corinthians 12:9, God promises, "My grace is sufficient for you, for my power is made perfect in weakness." Oh, how thankful I have grown to be for His grace and power! That is why I can wholeheartedly agree with Paul in this same passage when he says, "Therefore I will boast all the more gladly about my weakness, so that Christ's power may rest on me."

CHAPTER 10

When I said before that the incident with my teacher fit, it was not an immediate one. I mean, come on. It's inconceivable to think of anyone being capable of such a thing. I can't relate with a sexual attraction to children. I can hardly grasp the selfishness required to cross such a line. How could someone justify such disregard for another human being? What is worse, how can they get away with it? Yet our world is riddled with these realities and more. What fit was the extensive amount of pain and confusion I'd been carrying ever since I could remember. Although disturbing, the missing piece fell into place and the overall picture made more sense.

After I had recounted the details of that tragic experience, I had to leave the scene behind. I don't recall exactly how my viewpoint transitioned back to my current self, but the first grader and I were no longer one and the same. I had a lot to absorb and process. I needed to return to my safe place and gain some distance from it all. It had become obvious now that it was not safe to leave the first grader in this place anymore. Her small frame lay on the floor in front of me, curled up in a fetal position. I imagined scooping her up in my arms and took her with me. No bubble this time. We were simply free of that room, never to return again.

As we arrived through the billowy exterior of our safe haven, our second-grade self met us, showing great concern. She held on to my side with one hand while softly touching the little girl's leg as we crossed the tile floor. On the other side, I imagined the clouds to form a comforting bed. I gently laid the first grader down and tucked her in for some much-needed rest. The second grader stayed by her side. The scene was as soothing as I could imagine. There was really nothing else we could do.

The psychologist was concerned about rushing me back to reality, but we had already gone over time, and another appointment was waiting. He said some reassuring words about trusting what I had recalled to be real. We walked to the exiting waiting room, where he told me to take as much time as I needed. I'm sure that I looked quite shocked. I was numb. My mind was blank. I mean no questions or alarms were buzzing around. I wasn't rehashing the event I had just witnessed or rather endured. It was an eerie calm with an overwhelming amount of weight to it. I couldn't sit still. So I went to the ladies' room down the hall. It was empty as usual. I entered a stall and began sobbing uncontrollably for several minutes. Then I pulled myself together and left the building. I went on with the day's routine of picking up the kids and such, still in disbelief.

Fortunately, that same night, I already had a support meeting scheduled. Once again God had paved the way. It was vital for me to have a small group of ladies who had similar backgrounds with whom I could share the day's events. Even so, I waited until half way through our time together to open up. Then I just laid it out there. Their response was somewhat flat, but supportive. Some years later, one of the women confessed to me that she felt a little resentful because I appeared to be progressing quickly through things she had been struggling with for years. However, the group had served its purpose. I just needed a safe place to say my experience out loud and to begin the process of moving forward.

After the meeting, I felt somewhat better but still didn't want to go home quite yet. I'm not sure why. Maybe I simply needed more time to sort through things without the pressures of motherhood and wifely duties. I did call my husband to let him know that I wasn't returning right away. Then I drove to see a close friend in the next town over. It was a reflective, quiet drive as was my visit with her. My stay was short because she had a young family too. The psychologist also called to check on me. All in all, it was just the settling mix of comfort I needed to end my day.

The next week when I returned to image therapy, it all still seemed unbelievable. Yet somewhere deep within a definite calm relief was settling in. Again it is hard to put into words. It was somewhat like I had been holding my breath for years and now I had permission to breathe freely. There was an undeniable healing growing inside of me. When I tried to explain it to the psychologist, I put it in terms of percentages. In such a short time, by finally letting the truth out into the light of day, I felt about 90 percent unburdened. That may sound like a generous amount, but that's what my body was telling me. However, I also knew that there was a little more to uncover.

This knowing was so distinct that it could only have been from God. There was no wavering of my assurance. There wasn't any calculating by which I came up with an estimation. No one told me how quickly or slowly I should expect to feel better. I just was. On the outside, I still appeared frazzled and was extremely worn down. Like the first grader I had put to bed in the clouds, I would also require a lot of rest to fully get back on my feet, so to speak. But on the inside, where the greatest amount of turmoil had been brewing for so long, there was a huge sigh of relief. For the first time since I could remember, I began to feel peace stirring in my heart. Later, I described what I had been feeling as a blackness across my chest, blocking my heart and soul. It was a shroud of secret sin and shame. Even if it wasn't my own sin, the heavy burden had been laid on me. But now by grace it was completely gone and replaced by an endless path of hope, light, and peace extended heavenward. That's the image that came to me. With nothing holding me back any longer, the possibilities were endless.

However, there was a small yet vital portion of my childhood still veiled by the shadows. My instinct was to explore some of my earliest memories of a neighbor boy propositioning me. He was in fact a distant cousin who was four years older than my twin brother and me. His mother actually looked after us before we were old enough to start school. We even referred to her as our aunt. Because of our relation, our families spent lots of time together over holidays and summer cookouts. Now that I am an adult, I've become aware of some very dysfunctional behaviors in that family. As a child, though,

I didn't know any better. Once, this cousin showed the two of us an adult cartoon from one of his parent's nudist magazines. We were so young that we didn't get it in the least, but we knew they were naked, and it was secretive. As we grew older, this boy's attention to me increased. I remember our families even joking about a shotgun wedding someday. Unfortunately, our families' familiarity with one another allowed for some blurring of appropriate boundaries as we matured.

CHAPTER 11

There were two particular incidents with this cousin next door that clearly stood out in my memories. Once, we set up a tent between our two houses and thought an overnight campout would be fun. I guess our parents figured we were safe with this older boy, whom they considered family. I'm not for sure what age my brother and me were at the time. By my best estimation, we would have been in third or fourth grade, maybe the summer between. Of course, that would make the neighbor boy in seventh or eighth. The sleeping bags were laid out so that he was between the two of us. Once we had settled down for the night, the cousin opened his sleeping bag, facing me. He was completely nude and wanting me to look at him, hoping to make me excited, I suppose. I don't think my brother even knew what was going on from the other side of the tent. As I had always recalled it, I simply told him no and rolled over to face the other way. Then assumedly we fell asleep.

On another occasion not too long after, the cousin wanted to spend the night at our house with my brother. As with the tent, I had the same desire not to feel left out. So my parents let me make a pallet on the floor in my brother's room. I was all of the way across the room from the bunk beds, where the boys slept. Soon enough, the teenager slid out of the bottom bunk and down onto the floor beside me. This time, he asked me to have sex with him. Again I firmly said no and turned away from him. That's all I remembered. I just supposed that he went back to his bed and the matter was dropped. When telling the counselor about these events, he asked if I knew why the boy would even think I would want to have sex with him. I simply didn't know what would make him ask me that. These are the events as I had always remembered them. It wasn't the same as the empty gap of my first-grade year. These were solid memories of very inappropriate behavior. In my mind, I had emphatically stood up to this young man's unwanted advances. I had made my boundaries clear both verbally and physically. That's what I always believed and never thought to question. However, my next few sessions would reveal otherwise.

My instincts were telling me to further explore these moments in time. Also, we hadn't uncovered the mystery of the incident in which I felt hands holding me down. This was by far the most realistic and frightening sensory encounter that I had experienced. Therefore, I knew the touch of those hands must be linked to something disturbing. I needed to find out what exactly. I had noticed previously, though, that the fingertips of the hands were pointed toward my feat. This was odd, but I reasoned that the person attached to them had to have been facing that same direction. Therefore, it didn't seem likely that they could be the hands of an assailant. It was puzzling for a while but soon became clearer.

Visiting these two places in my mind was like when I became the first grader in the classroom. I viewed things through the eyes of my third grade self, but this time there was more of an emotional disconnect. I saw the shocking things that in actuality followed my refusals without suffering the fear and horror of it fully. In short, my older cousin did not accept no for an answer. In the tent, he even somehow coerced my brother into helping while he violated me. It was my sibling, as young and innocent as myself, that held my legs down. So my brother was facing away from the dastardly deed. I have no idea what he heard or felt during it. As an adult, I shared with him what I now recalled. He said that he didn't even remember the camping out or the sleepover. Nothing. I don't know how much he was aware of at the time, but I can certainly understand why his mind would want to block out any memories of those nights. I don't blame him in the least. I fully believe the cousin manipulated him into assisting.

Learning that there was more to these events than I consciously recalled all these years was somewhat surreal. I didn't experience quite the same sickening horror as with the first trauma. It was more like, somewhere deep inside, I had come to grips with the fact that something terrible had happened those two nights. I just needed to face it and acknowledge the reality to find closure. I didn't need to re-experience every little detail to convince myself, just enough to know for sure what had happened. Once I admitted to myself that I had indeed been raped, I was able to immediately detach and take a step back. Naturally, it was upsetting to a degree, but once I saw enough to confirm the inevitable outcome, I could set it free. Instead of focusing on the specifics, I saw the bigger picture. Once again, what I discovered fit like a long-lost puzzle piece. It made sense and lined up with the emotions I'd always struggled with. I could finally release the heavy burden of my clouded past and remember that I had already survived it.

Coming to grips with blocking out an entire memory was challenging. Although I hadn't given it much deep consideration over time, I was always aware that most of my first-grade year was a total blank. I have clear memories from as early as preschool and kindergarten and from second grade on but none of that particular year. It was strange, I'll admit, but it was part of my reality. Then I find out it was a purposeful omission. It is extremely difficult to comprehend keeping a secret from myself. Having personally experienced it, though, leaves little room for doubt, especially because of the tremendous healing it has brought me. My only disbelief is about how such atrocities happen, how someone can perpetrate such a heinous act, and wondering how I became one of the statistics. The response to these unanswerable questions is that God alone knows. He is the only one who can unravel and redeem such cataclysmic events. How repressed memories work is a marvelous mystery, as in I marvel at it.

Now I had to wrap my head around partial memory blocks from my past. Partial memories, at least the kind that I experienced, are an oddity in themselves. I don't know if the difference occurred because I was older when those things happened or that I had been formerly violated. Somehow, though, I could recall graphic details of each encounter right up until the horrible moment. Then, I just shut it off like a switch. It seems gullible to believe that my would-be attacker could simply be turned away by my refusal. However, that is what my mind chose to accept. I never dared to imagine any more had happened. Yet at this point in my therapy, I chose to explore it further. I believe my ability to confront these events was, at least in part, due to the strength rebuilding in me after the release of the first great trauma from my psyche. It may have also been possible partly because my mind hadn't guarded me from every detail early on. There must have been some suspicion wavering in my subconscious all those years. And after the counselor proposed questions concerning my recollection of them, I began opening up to the realization that something more probably happened in these episodes.

Looking back, it boggles my mind that I would put myself in either situation. I was young and naive. I don't recall feeling fearful or panicked about my cousin's advances, just disbelief and disinterest. I don't know why I didn't leave or tell my parents. In the tent, I was likely afraid to trek out into the dark. This may have been part of the boy's plan to isolate me. He sure seemed to have a lot more intended for the evening than we did. As for the occurrence in the bedroom, I realize it wouldn't have mattered if I had stayed in my own bed because our rooms shared a door between them. Once again, I now think the neighbor boy knew exactly what he was setting up. In all reality, I may have never stood a chance otherwise.

CHAPTER 12

For a while, I was hesitant to even share the details of my image therapy experiences. They are very personal and at some points disturbing. I have tried my best to shelter you from the unnecessary graphic descriptions. There are two compelling reasons to tell my story, however. One is my hope to encourage others who may be struggling with similar issues. The other is to glorify God. Second Corinthians 1:3–4 says it well: "Praise be to the God and Father of our Lord Jesus Christ, the Father of compassion and the God of all comfort, who comforts us in our troubles, so that we can comfort others with the same comfort we ourselves have received from God." It was the loving Father who meticulously brought me through it all. My healing is undeniable. God's presence throughout the journey was ever so faithful. And in His unmistakable character, He wrapped it all up with one beautiful symbol that will never escape me.

In the session that followed my final recollection, I once again began by entering my safe place. You remember, the white tile hospital like floor with billowing clouds surrounding on all four sides. It was empty and starved for décor, but I knew it was the only place that I was completely safe. Well, when I arrived on this day, there was a surprising new feature. In the middle of that cold, sterile floor stood a bubbling fountain. It was made of gray concrete with a slender pedestal base leading up to three narrowing tiers with curved detail edges. The only sound you could hear was that of the crystal clear water cascading down from one tier and spilling into the next. This beautiful sight was completely unexpected. It was joyful and refreshing, bringing a presence to the space of calm and hope. The sight of it caused me to draw in a deep breath and exhale in relief.

Any further details of the session escape me. I may have actually fallen asleep in the comfort. I recall waking up to the psychologist uttering my name. I felt embarrassed and apologized repeatedly. He assured me that it was all right and must have been what my body needed most.

That may have been my last session with the psychologist. There were more appointments made and cancelled for various reasons. Honestly, I just didn't feel the need to go back and uncover any more. The healing process wasn't over, but the triage was complete. The deep, dark desperation was gone. The shock was transforming into relief. The cancerous traumas of my childhood had been located and cut out. My description to everyone at the time was that it was like a shroud of heavy darkness had been lifted from my chest and now there was an endless path directly from my heart ascending up towards heaven. I hadn't been fully aware of the blocking shroud until it was gone. I guess it had been there so long; it was all that I knew. But now I felt amazingly light and free. I actually delight in God's timing once again here because just as my therapy sessions ended a new ladies study began at my church. It was a woman I had never heard of before named Beth Moore. The video series was titled *Breaking Free*. If you are reading this right now and don't know why that is significant, I greatly encourage you to do a little googling and find out for yourself. Not only was that study a godsend, it was a mountaintop experience for me. Since then, to date, I have done nine more of her Lifeway studies, heard her speak live on two occasions, and have read several of her books. I promise you will not be disappointed.

In one sense, I think about my fountain as a shiny bow that God wrapped my total experience up in, neat and tidy. But bows contain gifts, and gifts are meant to be opened. Whether you are the slow, careful, methodical kind or the rip-it-to-shreds kind of package opener, when the gift comes from our Heavenly Father, its enjoyment is meant to be savored and to last for a lifetime. Think about the rainbow. It was a magnificent sign to Noah that God would never destroy the earth by flood again. That promise doesn't carry the same kind of weight for us that it did for those who had just experienced such a cataclysmic event. Yet when I see one today, I still feel the warmth and love of our merciful Father. At the time that I am finishing this book, we just lost a dear friend to esophageal cancer. He was the patriarch of a large family and the life of the party. He was an elder at our church and a member of our Life Group. He visited the sick and was generous with all that he had. Besides his biological family, there are tons of us who feel like his family because that's the way he treated so many of us. On the day that our friend was diagnosed with cancer, their family received a strange, wondrous gift. There was a perfectly placed double rainbow directly over their house. The picture is spectacular.

In speaking with family members, I know that they were hoping it was a sign that he would be completely healed. We desperately prayed as a community and individually. We struggled with faith in the unseen and tried sincerely to center our hearts on "Thy will be done." As with any package, though, we can't know what's inside until it is revealed. Many of us had a precise vision of what we wanted this family's outcome to be. We selfishly did not want to lose this precious man in our lives. But we know that God's ways are not our ways and his knowledge is beyond our full understanding. We trust that He sees the bigger eternal picture that we cannot see. Sadly it became apparent that our loved one would not recover. But there was such a beauty in that family's surrender. They continued to praise God through it all and rejoiced through tears, knowing he was now with his Maker. So what was the meaning of their spectacular rainbow? We believe it was a sign reminding that God is with us and will never forsake us. Although His will was not our own, God was actively present in every moment. We won't know the full story until we all arrive home.

God's presence during a trial may sound like a generic interpretation of a gift. However, I know firsthand how important that reminder can be in a time of immense turmoil. Of course, others can speak this truth to us and we can read about God's promises in His Word. These are good, healthy practices for us to actively carryout in community with one another. How precious it is, though, when God Himself taps us on the shoulder with a very personal affirmation of

"I AM with you child." Sometimes this gift may come at the beginning of a season like when a prophetic friend delivered a message to me that "I was going to be delivered from it all." She knew nothing of my personal demons. I wasn't even searching yet for answers at that point. But when struggles began, I held on to that message like a lifeline. Similarly, when I cried out for help during my semiconscious experience with the invading sense of evil and the lighter sensation followed, that was a signpost I could return to over and over again for encouragement and strength. Other times, like with Noah's rainbow, gifts can come at the end of a difficult time. It can serve as a promise for the future, as with Noah, or simply mark a conclusion, something of a grand finale, if you will.

That's what I feel my fountain is, a grand milestone commemorating where God has brought me to. It is the pinnacle of my journey thus far. Yet this gift keeps on giving. Upon reflection, I find so much symbolism in the fountain. I believe its three tiers represent the trinity of Father, Son, and Holy Spirit. And it's no coincidence that it appeared in the center of my safe place because my security flows best when God is central in my life. The bubbling water spilling over reminds me of His Living Water imaged throughout the Bible. "And the LORD will guide you continually and satisfy your desire in scorched places and make your bones strong; and you shall be like a watered garden, like a spring of water, whose waters do not fail" (Isaiah 58:11, ESV). "But whoever drinks of the water that I will give him will never be thirsty again. The Water that I will give him will become in him a spring of water welling up to eternal life" (John 4:14, ESV). "For the Lamb in the midst of the throne will guide them to springs of living water, and God will wipe away every tear from their eyes" (Revelation 7:17, ESV). There are so many references to choose from, but one of my favorite depictions comes from the Psalms speaking of those who delight in the LORD. "He is like a tree planted by streams of water that yields its fruit in its season, and its leaf does not wither. In all that he does, he prospers" (Psalm 1:3, ESV). Just reading about it is refreshing.

Perhaps the most beautiful thing about my fountain is that it is always with me. All I have to do is be still, close my eyes, and imagine my safe place. I revisit it from time to time. Over the months and years directly following my image sessions, a progressive change took hold of my sanctuary. With each visit, I saw new signs of healing and growth. Grass began to grow in place of the tile floor. First, it sprang up between the cracks and stemmed out from the base of the fountain. It gradually sprawled out much like the roots of a tree; only these sprigs extended soothing water instead of drawing it up. Now it's a thick, luscious green carpet. The kind you want to walk on in your bare feet. Other signs of life came about too. Birds began to chirp and flit around in a joyful display. Later little yellow butterflies joined them, fluttering and floating around the waters of the fountain. Even the light itself, having been bright against the white tile, turned warm and luminous. Beams of sunshine came streaming in, initially through partings in the clouds. Now it peeks through vines and leaves that have grown around the edges like a trellis framing the space. It reminds me of an early morning or late afternoon glow, not too bright or too hot, just cozy and inviting with a gentle breeze flowing from west to east. It's a peaceful paradise to be sure.

CHAPTER 13

Immediately following image therapy, I would go back in my mind often to check on my younger self. It was a good barometer of how I was doing as a whole. For a very long time, the first grader continued to sleep and recuperate under her billowy covers. If you remember, I had put her in a bed that I imagined in the clouds around my safe place. I would be greeted by my second-grade self, and we would approach the side of the bed. At first she didn't stir at all. After a little while, she would sit up for just a minute then go back to sleep. This was a reminder for me to be patient with myself and to continue resting physically. Outsiders can impatiently assume that something is over and expect a person to just move on. Most had no idea what I had just been through nor understood its extent. I came to realize that twenty years of carrying such a heavy secret burden had been extremely taxing. It only made sense that full recovery wouldn't be immediate. I had to recognize and accept that complete healing would be a slower process than I wanted to admit. Likewise, I couldn't let other's expectations override what God and my body were telling me.

I want to be absolutely clear about my astounding recovery. It took several years to get to the place where I am now. It also necessitated a persistent search for self-awareness. Communication with my husband was key, although not always idyllic in the beginning. However, awkward interaction proved better than none at all. My instant concern was that he wouldn't love me anymore. I felt soiled, like damaged goods. Turns out that it didn't change the way he viewed me one bit. As a matter of fact, he was one of those "It's over, so move on" kind of people at first. There was some navigating that we both had to do as the healing process continued. I'm happy to say that now he is my biggest supporter. And as our communication continued to improve, so did the intimacy of our marriage (both in the bedroom and in everyday life).

I often struggled with frustration. Even I expected myself to improve at a tenacious rate. When depression or exhaustion would plague me once again, it seemed to come out of nowhere. My counselor had pointed out once that I often came to see him in the fall season. After contemplation, it made sense because that is when my greatest atrocity had occurred. Still, for a while, my husband had to remind me that it was a familiar pattern that would eventually pass. These phases weren't usually interruptive as much as just discouraging. I simply had to acknowledge them as part of the process. A couple of years ago, however, I was delighted when I realized that winter was approaching and I had not experienced a depression at all! It was liberating.

Again, to be crystal clear, I do continue to take medicine for depression. I've come to realize that I am prone to moods of melancholy due to a chemical imbalance. Medication allows me to be in control of the despair and sadness. I can choose to find the bright side or reach out to a friend rather than to isolate and slump into misery. There should be no stigma in seeking medical treatment or counseling. Some people only need this kind of help temporarily to get through a difficult period in their lives. Others like me benefit from a continuous dose to stabilize a biological irregularity that's genetic. With all that I've overcome, you'd think I wouldn't require a prescription to get by daily. Even I start to question its necessity, but every time that I try to wean myself off my medication, the results are the same. I simply function happier and healthier thanks to the wonder of science. Fortunately, I've found a remedy that works for me with limited to no side effects. If you are searching, I encourage you not to give up and to keep advocating for yourself because you are worth it.

One other unexpected pattern that I had to contend with came when each of my other two children entered their first-grade years. Like the previous one, I wasn't consciously aware of it at first.

I remember sitting in my counselor's office near the end of a session when it suddenly dawned on me. It had been three years since my true past was uncovered, and I was frustrated because this annual slump seemed worse than the last. Then it hit me like lightning. I simply said, "Oh my gosh!" The counselor asked, "What is it?" When I told him, we both agreed that it made perfect sense. Once again, part of the process. Still two years later, when my son was the same age, my husband had to gently remind me. Each time was less of a struggle than the one before, but it helped to recognize what was triggering old feelings. It was also good to have someone to acknowledge it with me.

When I first started checking on the girls back in my safe place, the second-grade me would show great concern for the resting first grader. As we stood at the bedside, she would look up at my face, scanning for a sign that all was going to be okay. Gradually, she became more self-assured. She would greet me at the near edge of the room as I entered, then grab my hand and skip as we crossed the floor. Eventually, my first-grade self began sitting up in bed, even smiling on occasion. I never pushed her to do more. My visits were simply ones of connection and caring. At first, she would tire out quickly. Then one day she was already sitting on the edge of the bed with her feet dangling over the side, happily conversing. Oh, did you think this thriving place would be reserved for only myself and the two younger selves? I mean, I didn't know what to expect either. But once the first grader got stronger, our oasis became a gathering place. It is now filled with happy chatter and visiting among girls of various ages. Everyone is cheerful and content. The atmosphere is lighthearted.

Again it is hard to explain without sounding strange, but they are all me. It's an assorted gathering of myself at different stages throughout my childhood. I don't know what any of them are conversing about. Maybe I could find out with more image therapy. I believe, however, that the point of this vision into my soul is to show the wholeness I now feel. It portrays the progression of health and wellness continuing to blossom at the core of who I am. I can only imagine that it is a result of getting to know myself better and having no more secrets. I knew communication was key to any relationship. I just didn't know that could include amongst my selves. I guess it makes sense, though. No more denial. No more disconnect. No more fantasy. Just honest love and grace filtered through my Heavenly Father's eyes.

The closest thing I've ever found to this indescribable picture in my mind is a scene from the movie *Lovely Bones*. The film itself was a little hard for me to watch. I didn't know beforehand the similarities it would have to my own story. There is a part toward the end, though, that I found greatly intriguing. It takes place in an expansive green meadow with a large beautiful tree in the middle. Basically, it's a gathering place in the afterlife for all the victims of a certain serial killer. Once this victim starts to accept what has happened to her, she comes to this place of eternal peace with others who have been healed of the same tragedy. Like my fountain, I believe the tree was to represent growth and healing. And the meadow was full of girls of all ages, frolicking together without a care in the world (or afterworld). I don't know that this example helps you to understand what I've experienced, but it was enthralling to me at the time. So I felt it was worth mentioning.

Besides the symbolism that I mentioned in the last chapter, the fountain in my gathering place also brings up a well-worn memory for me. It makes me recall the words of a familiar hymn growing up in church. "Oh Thou Fount of Many Blessings" was a standard in our congregation, as I'm sure it was in many. My fountain is a symbol of countless blessings I've received. Many of them during that year of recalling and processing my painful past. Weathering that year also opened my eyes to the years before when God faithfully protected me, gave me strength to endure, and prepared a path to redeem it all. It may sound contradictory to say that God protected me since I was violated at such a tender age. What I've come to understand is that others' free will can often intrude on my own. Not to be too simplistic, but it's true in every scenario of life. God's protection, however, can be seen in the way that I survived these intrusions. I've learned that repressed memories are actually a healthy coping mechanism that indicates strength. Although I felt weak and pathetic most of my childhood, it took a lot of courage to "hold it all together" and to keep moving forward. That was by God's design.

Honestly, I can look back on a lot of occurrences in my life that shine God's faithfulness. Questions that were answered instantly by divine knowing (the kind of knowing that permanently effects my view on life) or ones answered decades later. Prayers, both spoken and unspoken, fulfilled in His good timing. People definitely brought into my life for a certain time and purpose, as well as similarly using me in the lives of others. The longer I live the more experiences I have to look back on and God's presence is undeniable to me. He never forsakes us. He is always working for "the good of those who love Him." Even in the darkest of times, God is ready with a plan to comfort, sustain, heal, and redeem! One of my favorite verses comes from Joel 2:25, where God promises to "make up for all of the years that the locusts have stolen." Got any years that the "locusts" of evil have stolen from your life? It could be your own sinful choosing or something done to you by another. Either way, God is ready, willing, and incredibly able to liberate you from it and to begin a new thing in your life. I am living proof.

In a nutshell, that is why I want to share my story with the world. God's creative attention to details and to each one of us is amazing. The way that He took my empty, sterile safe place and turned it into a flourishing space of peaceful joy was an unexpected gift. I created the billowy environment to shelter me as I dealt with the harshest realities of my past. Moments so terrifying that only God could carry me through, something like "the valley of the shadow of death." All I could manage to do was to cling to the hem of His garment and try to trust. I couldn't begin to fathom what the journey would be like, let alone imagine life on the other side of healing. Yet I am sure that God had this fount of blessings waiting for me all along. Imagine His gleeful anticipation up until that moment. Time God spent consoling and strengthening me, sharing in my sorrows, all the while, knowing the beautiful gift He had in store. I guess that is what it's like concerning eternity too. Only God knows the extent of bountiful blessings awaiting His beloved in heaven. And He anxiously looks forward to the day it is all revealed.

CHAPTER 14

Suddenly finding my fountain coming from such a desolate place was a total surprise for me. I had not expected or anticipated it at all. In a way, the gift of heaven will be similar, beyond anything we can hope for or imagine. Yet we absolutely should be expecting wonderful things. Eternity is a gift that has been promised to us. We even get sneak peaks at times, although we don't always recognize them. Of course, the book of Revelation gives us some graphic images of the Second Coming that most of us stagger at processing. It can seem more terrifying than majestic. I like the way Jesus describes eternity, though, as the Father's house with many rooms prepared for us. That's comforting and inviting. However, I'm learning that there is more to be glimpsed and likened to our future experience in heaven. Things like unity in Christ, growing intimacy with God, and living in loving community are worth exploring here in the flesh before we receive their full unveiling in heaven. There is also testimony. I don't know about you, but I look forward to hearing every last soul's story of God's goodness in their life. I can't imagine it will ever get old. I have a lot to share too. And we've all got questions that we want answered, right?

I'm convinced more and more, however, that heaven is going to be full of small yet significant surprises like my fountain. Things of a very personal and joyous nature. It hadn't actually occurred to me until this very moment that we will continue to receive God's goodness throughout eternity. So we will have new testimonies to share endlessly. Excuse me while I "geek out" about that for a minute. It's a whole new concept that I had never considered before. I guess I think of my story as finite, confined to this world. But God is eternal and our souls are too. We were created for relationship with Him. Naturally, we will continue having interactions. Sorry, that may have been a revelation just for me. If so, then you understand where I'm coming from anyway.

Just like I can't fully conceive what the next few decades of my life will be like, I can't know for sure what eternity holds in store. I am sure, though, that it will be beyond my wildest hopes and dreams. I believe it with every fiber of my being because I have tasted God's goodness in this life. I've marveled at the way that everything He commands us to do is always ultimately for our own welfare. Forgiveness is a good example. Although it can be hard to pardon someone for wronging us, it's actually our self who is freed by the act. If we hold on to blame, the other person may be punished or they may not. It depends if they care or even know that they have hurt us. However, holding a grudge is always cancerous to the one nursing it. Essentially, resentment is perpetually reliving the harm done to us. Forgiveness is not excusing their behavior but rather preventing it from hurting us any further.

You may be curious to know whether or not I have forgiven my abusers from my childhood. The answer is yes. If for no other reason, I most definitely don't want to allow them to have any more control over my life. Their selfish actions have already stolen enough from me. Therefore, I defiantly move on. My greatest revenge is living a joyous, fulfilled life despite my hardships. For me there was no opportunity for prosecution or confronting my offenders. Too much time had passed, and there was no longer any physical evidence. The main thing that concerned me was that these people were no longer in a position to do the same thing to anyone else. Without going into specific detail, I feel confident that this is the case. Now I can't say that I have prayed for blessings upon their lives (that would be the ultimate test), but I have come to concern for their repentance. There is one point at which I can't help but feel compassion for all mankind and that is Judgment Day. I believe even the worst of us will tremble in God's presence. His wrath is something I cannot wish on even my worst enemy. Therefore, I honestly do hope that my abusers are brought to contrition before it's too late.

There are further illustrations of God's decrees being for our benefit. When we serve others, we often feel blessed in return. In this same way, we find it better to give than to receive. Reading God's Word produces revelation. Seeking His guidance leads to discernment. Pouring out our worship to Him results in filling us up with joy and confidence. So many of the woes we experience in life could be avoided if we simply followed God's commands to the letter instead of making up exceptions wherever we please. We too often choose to live precariously in the "gray area" rather than simply heed His words. I'm continually discovering new areas in which I struggle with this. But the longer I live, the more wisdom I perpetually see in every thoughtful instruction God gives us. His directives always lead to our welfare.

Now that my understanding of the Holy Spirit has started to grow, the fullness of Father, Savior, and Holy Presence is so precious to me. There is no aspect of life that our God cannot cover. He reaches to my innermost being and knows me better than I know myself. He is attentive to my heart's deepest desires and faithful to guide me in the direction I should go. He's lavish with His patience, love, and grace. God is relentless in His continual pursuit of us. There is no one more perfect for me. I am astounded by His infinite wisdom, and any little taste I receive of His glory leaves me in awe.

God is not in the business of manipulating us to cooperate with His will just because He wants His own way. Our Heavenly Father is deeply, sincerely invested in our well-being and happiness. Jesus's sacrifice on the cross is the greatest evidence of that. Our Creator loves us with a kind of lavish unconditional affection that we can only begin to comprehend. With devoted time and attention, however, we can practice receiving these gifts with greater awareness. The more I experience and recognize God's loving ways toward me in this life, I can't help but joyfully anticipate meeting Him face-to-face in the next. How can I look forward to a gift like heaven that has not been revealed yet? It's because I trust in the never-failing goodness of our God. Beloved, you can too.

"Blessed is the man who perseveres under trial, because when he has stood the test, he will receive the crown of life that God has promised to those who love Him" (James 1:12).

FOLLOW UP

As part of my continued journey earthbound, God has led me to another healing ministry. About nine years ago, our church began an extension of Celebrate Recovery, which originated at Saddleback Church in California. It's essentially a twelve-step program, much like Alcoholics Anonymous, but with a few key differences. Most importantly, we name our higher power confessing Jesus Christ. That is where all the authority for real change originates. Furthermore, it addresses all hurts, habits, and hung-ups, not focusing on only one addiction. I also like pointing out that "celebrate" is half of the CR name. Satan is masterful at undermining the good plans that God has designed for us. We are much too easily cheated out of giving ourselves credit for the little victories before the next trial or misstep comes along. This is where I realized the value of sharing testimonies.

There is so much to be gained by telling our stories to one another. It cultivates encouragement, strength, and communication, all of which the devil wants to deprive us of. Why? Because sharing also shines truth. We no longer have to believe the lies that no one else struggles or could understand. Nor do we have to fall prey to the traps of isolation and hiding our darkest secrets. In CR we often speak of not wearing any masks. This means owning up to our flaws and struggles, not pretending to have it all together while judging someone else. We practice accountability in small groups or between individuals with whom it is safe to share even our worst struggles. I personally have nothing about myself that at least one other individual doesn't also know. No one person knows everything. Yet by being open this way, the devil no longer has power to twist and manipulate me with fear and shame. I have found it to be a very liberating way to live.

Through CR I've started experiencing community more like the way I believe God intended it to be. Loving unconditionally, supporting without trying to fix one another, honoring healthy boundaries, and heavily leaning on Jesus Christ for guidance and strength. Right away our weekly meetings became a sanctuary for me where I was loved and accepted without conditions. Others appreciated me for my strengths and came to know my struggles. They never judged but lovingly encouraged me in my quest to overcome character defects. Whether I arrived upbeat or broken, they loved me the same. I realized it was something I was starving for. Pretty soon God nudged my heart to ask if my family enjoyed the same kind of sanctuary in our home. Wow, was that convicting! At the same time that I was learning to receive grace and mercy for myself, I became increasingly able to extend these same gifts to others.

One of the most essential elements of CR is a yearlong step study combining much scripture with well guided self-reflection and sharing. This is done in a smaller gender specific gathering. The timing once again was perfect for me. Because of all of the healing that had recently taken place, I wasn't searching for comfort in CR. What honestly drew me there was that I struggled with angry outbursts, especially at my children. I would go to bed many nights, crying and begging God to help me change. I love my kids so deeply, but no matter how hard I tried I couldn't control this ugly habit. The first thing we are challenged to come to grips with is that we are powerless to control our own tendencies and our lives are unmanageable on our own. What a relief not only to admit this but to acknowledge that the help we need comes from God alone. In our weakness, He is proven strong.

In His faithfulness, God did release me from angry outburst. However, He knew there was so much more I needed to uncover. During that first step study, He also loosened in me the grip of depression as my identity and living with a victim mentality. With all I had been through, I still wasn't aware that I functioned in life as a victim. Talk about an aha moment! And depression was something

I had barely dared to hope I might overcome someday, but I never knew how. It turns out that when the time was right, all I had to do was surrender. Depression is still something I struggle with from time to time, but it no longer defines who I am. It is not my identity! As I've participated in further study groups, He has continued to refine me in many unexpected yet relevant ways, one of which was the courage and discipline to write this book. I am so thankful to have the Heavenly Father, who cares for me in such a personal way. I'm also grateful that He has a plan for me to be a useful part of His greater design.

It's a beautiful thing the way God can take our past pain and use it in ministry to others. Even more astonishing is that He can use us to bless others no matter where we are in our own journey. I've heard it said before that God doesn't want our perfection, He wants our presence. If we can just get out of our own way by seeking Him through every season of life, God can still do miracles in and around us. That's what I'm learning. I'm still not perfect, which is humbling and a relief at the same time. Anything I accomplish is due to God's strength in me, not of my own merits. Yet I can accomplish great things, even in my brokenness, because He is so good. It doesn't have to be something grandiose like establishing a charitable organization or becoming a well-known author. If only one other hurting soul is offered a helping hand or simply reminded that God cares for them, that is enough. With God, the rippling effects can be tremendous.

Only The Beginning

The following is another testimony from this author.

The Marriage FORMULA

F—first God
O—open communication (honesty)
R—romantic gestures
M—money matters
U—understanding and unity
L—love for a lifetime
A—appreciate each other

One Valentine's Day, I got a surprising gift. It wasn't from my husband. It was from God. It had been a long tiring day, and it wasn't over yet. While I was resting my eyes to gear up for the evening, I felt a nudging inside me to praise God for the wonderful place that our marriage was at after twenty-one years. I've thought about this before, but this time, I felt the Spirit calling me to share it with others. So a conversation began in my head. First I thought, *What would I say?* Then I heard the Spirit answer, "Use an acrostic." I found this funny because a ministry I'm involved in called Celebrate Recovery uses those all the time. So then I asked, "What word would I even use?" The reply was instantaneous and surprising—FORMULA! I chuckled to myself. Then again I asked (in a rather snarky tone), "Okay, what would each letter stand for?" When I got the answer, I knew it was time to rein in my attitude and write some of this down. As I listened, God laid out exactly what I'm going to share with you. They are all valuable lessons that God has taught us through our marriage.

My husband and I were young when we married. We had just turned twenty-one and twenty-two a month before our wedding.

Looking back, we now realize that we spent just as much time getting to know our individual selves as we did each other in those early years. It never occurred to us that we could have used some help sorting through and setting right some of the "baggage" we had brought into our relationship—baggage like habits or patterns from our childhoods, specifically issues with anger, insecurities, and manipulation (guilt trips). There were also unresolved feelings about our dating years before meeting each other. We thought that we had put those to rest, but when the realities of day-to-day life started creeping in, the truth was revealed. Don't misunderstand; we were very much in love. Still we encountered some serious struggles early in our marriage. I'll share more details about these as we go, but that just makes the abundant place that we are now at in our relationship even more amazing. And all the credit goes to God.

First, God; second, your spouse; third, family.

As Christians, we kind of assume that God is a part of the equation. But there is a lot more to it than just having Him in your lives. Most lovebirds start out pretty obsessed with each other. Usually, things calm down eventually and they get into a comfortable pattern. It's similar with becoming a Christian. We're often excited about a new life in Christ, but the passion fizzles out quickly enough as we go about our daily living and lose focus on what truly matters most.

In our marriage, God has shown me three different times when I had started putting someone else before Him without even realizing it. First, it was my husband. Part of the baggage that I carried with me was a desperate neediness. I had no real self-esteem and depended on others to validate my worth, especially my husband. Not only was this overwhelming for him, but it also drew me away from a real relationship with God. I didn't consciously choose it. I would have never believed it if someone accused me of it. However, sure enough, as our struggles grew, the Spirit opened my eyes to the truth. I was shocked that I could do such a thing without even being aware of it. Ironically, in the next few years, I did it again with my children and then again with a close friendship. Thankfully, God made me aware of it each time. Of course, it was after much struggle in my life. But He was faithful and right in doing so.

In any relationship, priorities can easily get out of whack. The more intimate the bond, the more easily boundaries can become blurred. That's why we have to actively seek God first. Not just attend church regularly, but also cultivate a close personal dependence on Him. A funny thing about God is that everything He asks us to do "for Him" is always what is best for us. Growing our connection with God helps us to become more Christlike in our relationship with our spouse. Maturity in Christ helps provide strength in trials, guidance in times of decisions, and it creates overall peace in our lives whatever the circumstances we face. Seeking a personal relationship with God and sharing it with one another also creates intimacy between spouses. This order is critical to maintaining balance and harmony in any marriage.

We learned another lesson during one of our most painful times of struggle. Our marriage had been devastated by unfaithfulness. We were working opposite shifts at the time and didn't see much of each other. The time we were together was hectic, adjusting to being first-time parents. Pressures and relationships outside of our own were demanding our attention and increasingly winning. Let me tell you that the devil never misses an opportunity. Just when you think you're handling everything the best you can, evil can step in with a most enticing disguise. There is a Bible verse to that effect in 1 Corinthians 10: "If you think you are standing firm, be careful that you don't fall."

It truly is a miracle that our marriage survived at all, let alone now flourishes. Fortunately, what evil determines for our destruction, God can and will use for His greater good. With this trial, there were many revelations. One in particular relates to the topic of order. Ready for it? Every one of us is a child of God above all else, even being a spouse. Shocking, I know. It sounds so obvious, but in the throes of pain and agony caused by someone we love, the concept can be easily overlooked. What we learned was that although God cares deeply about the pain caused, He also has a higher agenda and something to teach each person involved. There were times in our situation when neither of us believed finding happiness again was possible. Yet two more kids and all these years later, we are so thankful for all God did to accomplish exactly that.

Open Communication

Honesty between two people is only possible if both remain open to listening and to discussion. When communication breaks down in any relationship, it inevitably leads to misunderstandings. At "best" it causes loneliness and distance between us. At its worst it becomes an open invitation for the devil's evil schemes. God created us for community with others and Himself. It's a deep need within us. If that need is being neglected in one area, we tend to seek it in another. It's like trying to satisfy my need for God through my husband, kids, and friends at various times. It's also a big reason for unfaithfulness. This can be an emotional betrayal but so often involves the physical as well.

God created sex as a gift of pleasure and as a lasting way to bond two people together for the long term. Most people, even Christians, don't define sex within the confines of marriage anymore. It's pretty much accepted that physical intimacy cannot be avoided. People are expected to be ruled by and give in to their sexual urges. So why is society so shocked when it invades a marriage? For years, I've struggled to reconcile God's purpose for sex against the grotesque distortion the world has created. Then someone explained it to me like this: sexual intimacy is the closest thing we know on earth to the intense connection we will feel with God in heaven someday. In other words, it's a foreshadowing of closeness and joy awaiting us there. Admittedly, this can be an awkward thought to follow, but as soon as I heard it, the whole thing made perfect sense. If genuine intimate connection (sex) is this precious, of course, the devil would be so active in trying to confuse and poison our understanding of it!

This is a topic that could fill a book in itself. For our purposes here, though, it's just one example of how poor communication can affect a marriage. We can't ignore an innate need for long without some form of consequence. For my husband and me, conversation started out as one-sided most of the time. If not, then it was loud and unhealthy. Things left unsaid often came out eventually in a much harsher, more hurtful way. Another thing we realized through our struggles was how crucial it is to truly understand each other. We also experienced the joy of being understood. No more wishing the other could read our mind or discussing private matters with outsiders. This just leads to misunderstandings and hurt feelings and draws a couple away from each other. Instead, choose to talk to each other in love and gentle honestly.

Another thing that we do much better now is seeking spiritual guidance. Couples should make decisions together, but they aren't always going to agree. Over time we've learned the best way to honor one another is through prayer and compromise. It's also been our experience that God's direction can be trusted. At times, He has laid some heavy changes on my heart that my husband had no interest in. Sometimes the compromise was not to act right away. Then God would make it clear to me that action was what He wanted. So I would say to Him, "Okay, but You have to get my husband on board." The first time, I was sure revisiting a subject that had already been tabled would cause tension. But I was amazed to discover that my husband's heart had been changed. Now I simply trust that if God wants us to do something, He will make a way. The beauty of it is that we can both feel free to share our deepest feelings, make decisions together without fear, and then know with confidence that God is in control.

Romantic Gestures

It's important to keep the spark alive if we want a happy marriage. One way is to learn each other's "love language" and apply it often. What says "I love you" to one person may not say the same thing to another. I used to buy my husband books about men living Christian lives and plaques saying things about being a great dad. After years of dusting piles of untouched books, I finally got the message. My spouse hates reading, and there's only so much wall space for all those plaques. I don't think he reads those either. It's not rocket science, just a matter of paying attention to what makes the other person feel known and brings a smile to their face.

Another way to keep the fire burning in a romance is to reconnect to the feelings that drew you together in the first place. When we went to our first visit with a marriage counselor, we were in a state of devastation. So it was surprising to find ourselves reminiscing about the way we met after just a few minutes. Looking back, I think the counselor was trying to demonstrate that there were still feelings to be rekindled between us. He actually said that our marriage could be even better than it ever was. I remember this vividly because it made me furious at the time. How could this destructive wrong make anything better? It took several years before I understood that he was right. The point is that if the simple sharing of how we met could bring smiles to our faces that day, it is truly powerful stuff. So we make it a regular practice to visit shared memories. We laugh together, play together, and celebrate the good times we've shared.

There is one more thing that we've learned about keeping the romance alive in our marriage. That is to respect each other by guarding against the deterioration of our love together. The world offers a lot of distractions that can lead too easily down a destructive path. Pornography is a big problem in our society. Its availability is too great. And a surprising number of couples reason that it's okay if it's watched together. Some wives make excuses for their husbands and tell themselves that looking is harmless. However, Ephesians 5:3 says, "There must not even be a hint of sexual immorality, or any kind of impurity." Other harmful sources of entertainment are equally available and less taboo. Movies are one example. Personally, we've made the choice to almost never watch anything R-rated based on the knowledge that once an image is seen, it can't ever be erased. There are so many things that I wish I had never seen.

My husband still enjoys a little action-violence now and then, but it's almost impossible to avoid nudity or very provocative scenes anymore. When we were first married, he would insist that it was just part of the story and no big deal. (Sound familiar to anyone?) I would argue that even if he didn't think it caused him to be tempted, it definitely made me feel devalued. We went back and forth like that for years—until one movie was so blatant about throwing a nude sexual fantasy scene in between two fighting montages that even he couldn't find a sliver of a connection to the plot. Ha! So now when something objectionable pops up, we simply turn our heads to meet each other's gaze instead. It may seem like a small gesture, but it's meaningful enough that we usually end up in a kiss. Even our twelve-year-old son has learned to overt his eyes at times. I think our future daughter-in-law will appreciate that trait in him when the time comes.

Having children has caused us to set our standards even higher. PG-13 isn't what it used to be. Maybe it never was actually. When we were kids, though, evening television was family time. Now it seems there is nothing we can feel comfortable watching together. It isn't just about nudity either. Arguing is portrayed as funny. Spouses don't respect one another. And promiscuity is a part of normal everyday life, sometimes starting as young as junior high. Don't even get me started on commercials these days. In my opinion, Victoria's Secret (which in truth is no real secret anymore), Hardees (with their sensual sale of "meat"), and others like them are paving the way for society's mass destruction. I warned you not to get me started. I am thankful for the technology of parent controls and blocking certain temptations. However, it's a sad thing when even Saturday morning cartoons get filibustered.

Money Matters

In real estate, they say the three keys to success are location, location, location. Well, in money matters, the secret to success is agreement, agreement, agreement. There are probably a million different ways that a couple can go about handling their finances. The how isn't as imperative as establishing some agreed-upon guidelines early on. There is not right or wrong way as long as there is understanding about the way things will be done. It may seem like something that will just work itself out, but money can be a big source of marital tension and stress. One thing good to agree on is how much one person can spend without consulting the other. This revelation probably occurred after an unfortunate purchase or two. I really don't remember, but somewhere along the way, it proved to be significant for us. So we take advice from Philippians 4:2, which encourages believers to "agree with each other in the Lord."

Actually, for us a lot of issues did "fall into place" without much discussion. I am definitely better at keeping the checkbook and paying the bills on time. Responsibility is one of my good traits. My husband, on the other hand, actually understands numbers much better than me and tends to get less overwhelmed. That's why he is in charge of handling our taxes every year. We both worked in the beginning but have come to value my time more at home. During the years of rebuilding our then-broken marriage, stress weighed heavily on me. With kids and working full-time, not only did the housework suffer, so did my parenting. I began to realize that my best efforts were all going to my job and that my family got the leftovers. Even working part-time left me easily frustrated and quick to lash out in anger.

Also while we were both working, an odd pattern of competition emerged. When I would complain about my awful day, I would often hear the words, "You don't know what tough is. My job is much worse than yours." Chalk it up to immaturity or poor listening skills, but the result was the same. We both were left feeling unappreciated, unheard, and no less stressed. We might still be stuck in that pattern, if it weren't for the Spirit's intervention. You see one of the first leadings that I truly recognized was one telling me not to work anymore. Needless to say, that didn't go over too well at first. But God was persistent about it with me. While sitting in church service one morning, I heard the preacher say, "Maybe we don't want to hear what the Spirit is telling us because then we might have to act on it." My heart immediately cried out, "Yes, I do want to hear!" And instantly the Spirit responded, "Then how can you ignore Me when you fully know what I'm wanting you to do?" Right then I was convicted. I wasn't looking forward to another heated argument with my spouse, but I had great peace knowing I was doing the right thing. So we discussed it some more and decided to step out in faith.

What we discovered might surprise some. We realized that we each have a few God-given desires that were being shortchanged. For him, basically, it's a need to be taken care of domestically. What he wants most is support, encouragement, and a little pampering. Having dinner ready and a warm welcome when he gets home are important to him. These were all things I had little energy to provide, however, after working all day myself and caring for the kids. I also felt guilt for being weak and unable to "do it all" like I perceived others could. Once staying home, though, I actually enjoyed doing these things, and the stress was a lot less for everyone. My family finally got my best efforts first, and we were all happier for it. Now that our kids are older, I do work part-time again. However, my hours are flexible so that I can still serve my family's need first and balance between work and sanity are a number one priority.

One of the deep desires that I discovered in myself was similar to my husband's. I have a need to be taken care of too. It's more like being provided for, though, and also protected. I'm perfectly capable of earning a living and fending for myself, but I feel a greater fulfillment not doing it all alone. It's kind of like having a knight in shining armor except I know that I'm not helpless and I don't act like it either. My husband takes care of me because he wants to and I enjoy it. Of course, I'm not just sitting around, eating bon-bons all day. The amount of effort that we each put into our home and family are equal; they're just different. They also complement or complete one another. While my husband is a diligent, hard worker, my skills fall more in the emotional and spiritual realms. Yet we both pitch in wherever and whenever needed. I earned some money from odd jobs arranged around our kids' busy schedules. He coached their sports teams and planned quality time with our family like camping and road trips. He's even been known to help around the house now and then. Best of all, everyone benefits. Working together as a team this way brings peace to our home. It also creates intimacy between us as a couple.

We are not advocating that women shouldn't work or that men have to be "the breadwinner." What we are simply saying is that it might be beneficial to consider the way that God created us unique, both male and female, as well as individuals. We shouldn't be afraid to take an honest look at the deep desires within ourselves. It may result in some changes, like it did for us. Or it may only confirm that things are good just the way they are. What's invaluable is that we talk it over, be self-aware of our own needs as well as those of our spouse, and be sure these needs are being met no matter our situation.

Understanding and Unity

Over the course of a marriage, there will be many seasons of life to be faced. We haven't experienced them all yet, but there is one thing that we have learned. Each season alters the relationship somehow. It's vital for the health of a marriage to apply some grace and understanding as these changes affect the way we relate. In the beginning, things are mostly romantic, and it's not hard to focus on each other. Then there is a time of sacrifice as we begin to acquire things and work toward future goals. Some of the focus shifts to career building, buying a home, building up savings, etc. For many, there comes a season of parenting. Having a baby and starting a family can be wonderful, but it is also a lot of change. There is less sleep but more energy exerted. The younger years can feel socially isolating and physically over stimulating. The pressure to provide increases. There are additional issues of discipline, education, and spiritual nurturing to attend to. Either spouse can easily end up feeling neglected. It may seem at times like we're being pulled apart by life.

Personally, we found it essential in times like these to remember that we are not each other's enemy. Unity means that, no matter what the circumstances, we work through them together as a team. It's so beneficial to have someone to count on, to lean on when times get tough. That doesn't mean that we won't let each other down from time to time. We are only human after all. That's where grace comes in. We know each other well enough to talk through the disappointments, offer forgiveness, and make amends when necessary. Don't let misunderstandings go too long without sorting them out. There are enough battles to be fought out in the world. Why be at war with each other at home? Understanding means taking a step back and seeing the bigger picture in times of struggle. We try to identify the real source of the stress. Then we go to God and each other for encouragement to get us through. We also take comfort in remembering that this phase won't last forever. "There is a time for every-thing and for everything there is a season" (Ecclesiastes 3:1).

In our journey, we have entered the next stage of life. As our kids have grown, we find more chances to reconnect as a couple. Date nights are less complicated since we don't need a babysitter any-more. Sometimes they are even spontaneous when our kids all go out or spend the night with friends. That brings up another lesson we've learned—don't waste an opportunity. That doesn't mean we have to go out on the town (or whatever they call it these days). Sometimes the reality of getting older means we just need some "down time" to relax. What's important is that, no matter how we choose to spend our time, we choose to do it together, and we make it count.

One example of this for us, believe it or not, is texting. So often throughout the day, I think warm, fuzzy thoughts about my husband. However, by the time we both get home, we're exhausted, and those feelings have faded away due to the busy demands of life. What's great to me about texting is that I can send a message while it's fresh in my mind without worrying about interrupting his busy day with a phone call. He doesn't have to be free to talk but can respond when he gets the chance. This greatly improves our communication and our flirting. We've been doing this for so long that much can be conveyed simply through emojis now. Texting makes us feel more connected throughout the day which helps keep continuity in our relationship despite the scattered remoteness of our daily routines. In other words, we may still be exhausted when we return home at night, but nothing gets left unsaid. Instead of feeling like we have to catch up, homecoming is more welcoming and affectionate.

Eventually, we know that this interval of reconnecting will lead to what most refer to as the "empty nest" point of our lives. When our oldest started college, we began experiencing what it was like let-ting the little ones fly from the nest. It actually starts way back with kindergarten and greatly intensifies with the addition of driving and dating. There is just something unnatural about watching our "baby" drive away in the car by herself for the first time. I swear it felt like a physical "cutting of the apron strings," as people say. On the other hand, it did go a long way in preparing us for the even bigger step of her going away to school. At this time, our oldest is now married (yet another major but mostly joyous change), and our second daughter is living in her own apartment. Our youngest, a son, is a senior in high school. Though we are close, I still can't quite comprehend what it will be like to have them all out of the house or how I will feel about it. The good thing, though, is that my husband and I are confident in the connection we share. Their absence will change the dynamics in our home but not the way that we feel about each other.

We got a small taste of what this might be like on our fourteenth wedding anniversary. It was a belated tenth-anniversary trip and the first time that we had been on vacation without the kids since they were born twelve years earlier. This fact hadn't even occurred to us until after we arrived at our hotel. We had a wonderful time. God blessed us with sights of beauty and adventures filled with joy. It was a bit like rediscovering the kid in both of us. We even joked that it was good to know that we still enjoyed each other's company after all these years. Although we did miss the kids, it was a notable health check of our connection to one another. We passed with flying colors.

There is another stage that we have not yet reached but have witnessed our parents and several friends go through. At a certain age, the tables of life turn and children become caretakers for their parents. This season can be very stressful on all parties involved. It also involves moments of painful loss and sorrowful goodbyes. However, this phase can be coupled with another kind of care taking that brings a lot of unbridled joy. We hear that babysitting one's grandkids is a chance to relive the love and laughter of parenting with none of the heavy responsibilities. I, for one, really miss my kid's younger years. That is to say I miss the cooing and snuggles, not the sleepless nights or potty training. I look forward with great anticipation to the day that my babies have babies of their own. However, I've already prepared myself for the inevitable fact that Grandpa will be known as the fun one. That's okay, though, grandmas are lovable by definition. Feel free to look it up.

Of course, this isn't an exhaustive list of everything a marriage can encounter along the way. There are a few that we've been through that are unique to ourselves and God's plan for our particular lives.

Sometimes unexpected things can come back to haunt us from our childhood or past. Serious illnesses, tragic events, and unrealized dreams are a few more. Whatever each of our paths, thankfully, God has it all in hand. He is ultimately in control even in the hard times. Meanwhile, we need to be mindful of the ways that different seasons in life can influence the bond between us. We must remember to lean on each other and take comfort in God's caring love for us. As long as we do, we can weather any phase that life throws our way.

Love for a Lifetime

We should go into marriage fully committed to the concept of "till death do us part." There are many vows that a couple can make on their wedding day, but we think one of the most critical one is promising to love each other for our whole lives. It seems like too many people these days go into marriage with a wait-and-see mentality. Still others avoid the official institution altogether, keeping a quick and easy escape route available should they choose to use it. We are not talking about staying in an abusive situation or living out a loveless marriage. But we have to be careful not to buy into society's idea of such disposable unions.

My husband and I certainly intended to spend the entirety of our lives together. Yet when our relationship hit rock bottom, we still considered divorce as an option. Fortunately, for us, it was definitely a last resort, and the child we already had together weighed in heavily. Still, there were moments for both of us when it looked inevitable. It's only by God's grace and continually seeking His strength and guidance that we made it through those very hard years. It wasn't an overnight fix or just one thing that helped our marriage heal. There were many ups and downs. The one constant, though, was God's faithful leading. As long as we continued to seek, He kept us heading in the right direction.

However, even after much counseling and resolving to work things out, we struggled to feel "in love" again. We doubted that God would truly want us to live out the rest of our years together that way. So we asked Him to show us how to fall in love again. I don't remember if it was days, weeks, or months before we received an answer, but God came through loud and clear. He led us to a program called His Needs, Her Needs (formed by Joe Beam based on a book of the same name written by Dr. William F. Harley). It was exactly what we needed to get us to the next stage of healing in our relationship and in ourselves. While facilitating and working through the program, we saw God at work in our own relationship and in others. The results weren't always a fairy-tale ending, but we saw His wisdom in the material. It focused each of us on our own behaviors and taught us to trust our significant other to be doing the same. Of course, this takes two willing and active participants. It also takes time. I would say that this program was a key factor in developing our open communication and appreciation of each other.

One concept that cannot be ignored when talking about love is the unconditional kind. This is the type of affection God offers to every one of us and wants us to show to others. What better place to practice this than at home with those closest to us? God understands that we are weak and will mess up sometimes but is always willing to forgive a repentant heart. Although He may not always be happy with our choices or behavior, He continues to love and want what is best for us. He also speaks truth and guides us, often more gently than we deserve. God continually reminds us whose we are and what we are called to be. In order for us to practice unconditional love in our relationships, we need to remind ourselves of these great blessings daily. Then out of our thankfulness, practice these traits with others. There is a saying I came across a few years back that I find to be a good metaphor for marriage. "If the grass seems greener on the other side, water your grass!" (unknown).

Appreciate Each Other

Last but by no means the least, it's important to show our appreciation for each other. I mentioned before the good thoughts I have about my husband throughout the day. So often we can think about the things we esteem in one another, but neglect to share them. We tend to assume that our spouse knows how we feel. That may be true, however, we all enjoy a little recognition now and then. We shouldn't just think good thoughts. We need to share them out loud with our spouse and to others. This remedies the common ailment of feeling unappreciated, which easily occurs in various areas of our lives. Everyone wants to be valued and validated. We've found that we never get tired of hearing it either.

I have always been thankful for the way that my husband works hard and takes care of our family. But when I am not working outside of our home, it means even more to me. One of the ways that I try to support and encourage him is to tell him often what it means to me. I share with him the way it makes me feel and acknowledge the effort he puts forth. This can be especially uplifting after a particularly hard day. Likewise, my husband recognizes my endeavors at home and with the kids. It's not a case of "I said something nice about you. Now it's your turn to complement me." We both share from a place of sincere, heartfelt gratitude, and love for the other person.

As parents, we discovered a unique way to go about this with our kids too. A counselor told us to keep some colorful marbles in a jar displayed in a common area of the house. Whenever one member of our family did anything we appreciated, we were to tell them to take a marble from the jar and place it in a second one. Then once the second jar was full, we would celebrate with a family activity. Our kids loved this routine! They found a special rainbow-colored bowl to hold some colored glass stones we found in the candle isle of the store. I also purchased a clear vase that we could see the stones through as it filled up. A common saying in our home became "You can put a stone in for that." Sometimes we forgot how crazy that might sound to guests that were over, so we had to explain ourselves once in a while. We even expanded the gesture to include some of our friends who came over often. They knew that putting a stone in was a renowned symbol of recognition and enjoyed it as much as we did. It really is an honor just to be nominated.

It just goes to show that everyone like to be appreciated. One more thing that I have noticed, more than my husband, is how we can seek esteem from others through humor. The reason I can identify so readily with this concept is because of years spent feeling like my spouse got laughs at my expense. I was often left feeling publicly humiliated, as well as, depreciated. Of course, he saw this as harmless fun. After much discussion (and periodic reminders), however, we now have an understanding that I do not want to be used as material for his personal comedy hour. He tries to respect the way that it makes me feel devalued even if he doesn't agree with it. I appreciate his consideration of my feelings. It may just be a point of contention for us, but it's still a valid example of showing respect and love for another.

One final note about appreciation is that a marriage relationship is something to be treasured. Because of the struggles that we've overcome, we are more thankful than ever for the special gift that God has given us. I fully believe that the place of abundance we now enjoy is so close to what Adam and Eve felt for each other before sin came into the world. Beyond that, I can only imagine what it must have been like in the ideal surroundings of Eden and to be in the close personal presence of our Creator. What we have discovered, though, is that marriage can be so much more than most of us dare to dream of, even in this imperfect existence of ours. If we open ourselves up to the possibilities of God's imagination and refuse to settle for earthly ideas of good, the union of marriage can be like the pearl of great price. Its worth is beyond measure, something that merits our labor and protection. We hope that our relationship can be an example for our children and grandchildren someday. That it will raise the standard by which they measure their future relationships. If so, maybe they will get a head start on experiencing the wonderful plan that God intended between a husband and wife.

You've probably already noticed that none of these concepts stand alone. They all overlap and weave together. No one single act can keep a marriage united independently. However, interwoven throughout the fabric of our daily lives, they work conjointly to maintain the strength and health of a relationship. Then when stressors of life weigh us down, we have something sturdy to fall back on. We are told in John 16:13 that "in this life we will have many trials and sorrows" but that we can "take heart because I [Jesus] have overcome the world."

Despite a long list of struggles that we have encountered throughout our lives, God has proven Himself faithful in walking along side us for the journey. We have personally experienced His comfort, guidance, discipline, grace, unconditional love, and blessings. We can bear witness to the truth of Romans 8:28, which says, "We Know that in all things God works for the good of those who love Him." Evil will always be trying to divide and conquer is in our families, marriages, churches, and nations. So I get flat out excited when the Spirit reveals the devil's plans for what they are (distortions of the truth) and equips us to overcome. For years as things improved in our marriage, I was thankful, but neglected to praise God publicly for what He has done. A voice of doubt would say things like "What if you mess up tomorrow?" "What if your marriage proves not to last?" "If you declare victory now, you and God will look foolish if you falter or fail in the future." Unfortunately, I listened to those lies for way too long. By doing so, I allowed evil to rob us of joy and encouragement we could have been sharing with others. Worst of all, I wasn't praising God enough.

However, this time the voice was finally refuted, and I found the strength needed to step out in faith and act. The Spirit reminded me that it's not about our performance. No matter what comes, the amazing truth is that the things God has taught us are no less true! If we fail, it will be because of poor choices we make. If our marriage fails, it will be because we quit following the "formula" God laid out for us. God's wisdom is true throughout the ages. So we are able to celebrate with confidence the many blessings He has given us. It brings even greater joy to our relationship when we do. Hopefully, sharing this story will inspire and encourage other relationships wherever they are in their journeys. Most importantly, though, we give all the glory to our Heavenly Father, whose love knows no end. He is worthy of our praise! How great is the Father's love for us, vast beyond all measure. May we all experience it deeply so that it spills out into our marriages, to those around us, and into the world. Amen.

About the Author

A uthor D. T. Christian grew up in a small town just outside of the St. Louis area. She earned a bachelor's degree in early childhood education from Missouri State University. She now resides in Springfield, Missouri, with her husband, two cats, and one dog. The other loves of her life are her three grown children, who still affectionately refer to her as Momma. She and her family enjoy spending time outdoors, camping, hiking, and experiencing God through nature. They also like playing board games and watching movies together. In her spare time, DT takes pleasure in scrapbooking all their adventures and special moments growing up. Similar to writing, however, this is always a continual work in progress. Worship and intimacy with the Father are what rejuvenates and gives DT strength for navigating this life. It was His calling that brought upon this book and His passionate faithfulness that inspires her to share her story.

CPSIA information can be obtained
at www.ICGtesting.com
Printed in the USA
BVHW082140040220
571444BV00001B/119